Enforcing Employer Sanctions

Challenges and Strategies

Michael Fix
Paul T. Hill

May 1990

The RAND Corporation
JRI-04

The Urban Institute
UI Report 90-6

ENFORCING EMPLOYER SANCTIONS
Challenges and Strategies

Published jointly by

The RAND Corporation
1700 Main Street
Santa Monica, CA 90406

The Urban Institute Press
2100 M Street, NW
Washington, DC 20037

Library of Congress Cataloging in Publication Data

Enforcing Employer Sanctions
Challenges and Strategies / Michael Fix and Paul T. Hill

1. Alien labor--Government policy--United States.
2. Alien labor--United States--Criminal provisions.
3. Emigration and immigration law--United States--Criminal provisions. I. Hill, Paul Thomas, 1943- .
II. Program for Research on Immigration Policy (U.S.)
III. Title.

HD8081.A5F58   1990   90-12280
331.6'2'0973--dc20   CIP

ISSN 0897-7399
ISBN 0-87766-483-8
ISBN 0-87766-482-X (casebound)

Distributed for
The Urban Institute Press by

University Press of America
4720 Boston Way
Lanham, MD 20706

Also available from

The RAND Corporation
1700 Main Street
Santa Monica, CA 90406

ENFORCING EMPLOYER SANCTIONS

Challenges and Strategies

Michael Fix and Paul T. Hill

Program for Research on Immigration Policy

The RAND Corporation
Santa Monica, CA

The Urban Institute
Washington, D.C.

The RAND Corporation was chartered in 1948 as a nonprofit institution to "further and promote scientific, educational, and charitable purposes, all for the public welfare and security of the United States of America." To meet these objectives, RAND conducts rigorous analyses of significant national problems to provide decisionmakers and the public with a better understanding of the policy issues involved.

RAND's research is analytic, objective, and interdisciplinary. National security programs focus on the planning, development, acquisition, deployment, support, and protection of military forces, and include international matters that may affect U.S. defense policy and strategy. Domestic programs include civil and criminal justice, education and human resources, health sciences, international economic studies, labor and population, and regulatory policies.

The Urban Institute is a nonprofit policy research and educational organization established in Washington, D.C., in 1968. Its staff investigates the social and economic problems confronting the nation and government policies and programs designed to alleviate such problems. The Institute has two goals for work in each of its research areas: to help shape thinking about societal problems and efforts to solve them, and to improve government decisions and performance by providing better information and analytic tools.

Through work that ranges from broad conceptual studies to administrative and technical assistance, Institute researchers contribute to the stock of knowledge available to public officials and private individuals and groups concerned with formulating and implementing more efficient and effective government policy.

ACKNOWLEDGMENTS

The authors' debts are many in the writing of this report. First, we would like to express our thanks to the excellent work of The RAND Corporation and The Urban Institute staff who were part of the joint project teams that examined IRCA's implementation and on whose work this report draws. These include Susan Gonzalez Baker, Jason Juffras, Julie Goldsmith, Wendy Zimmermann, Demetra Nightingale, and Regina Yudd of The Urban Institute, and Lorraine McDonnell, Abby Robyn, Elizabeth Rolph, Patrick Murphy, David Menefee-Libey, Lin Liu, and Kathi Webb of The RAND Corporation.

We would also like to acknowledge the advice given us by the manuscript's many insightful readers. These include Frank Bean, The Urban Institute; Richard Day, Committee on the Judiciary, U.S. Senate; Deborah Hensler, The RAND Corporation; Jay Jennings, the General Accounting Office; George Peterson, The Urban Institute; Peter Schuck, Yale Law School; Al Stapleton, The General Accounting Office; and Georges Vernez, The RAND Corporation.

We are especially indebted to Joan Allen of The RAND Corporation who produced and generally improved the document.

Finally, we are indebted to the many respondents who shared their time and insight so generously over the course of this project.

CONTENTS

Tables

Figures

This study is part of a broader two-year study of the implementation of the 1986 Immigration Reform and Control Act (IRCA) undertaken by the Program for Research on Immigration Policy.

The study examines the implementation of the key IRCA provisions affecting employers. IRCA forbade employers to hire illegal aliens, and established a public information and regulatory apparatus both to help employers comply with the law and to detect and punish violators. The study is based on extensive interview and other data collected between February 1988 and November 1989 in Washington, D.C., the four regional offices of the Immigration and Naturalization Service, four state capitals, and eight localities. The study concludes that the implementers have essentially met the challenges of IRCA's first three years. It also concludes, however, that the arrangements that were adequate for the start-up phase would be seriously inadequate for a more mature program.

The Program for Research on Immigration Policy was established in February 1988, with initial core funding from The Ford Foundation, to provide analysis that will help inform immigration and immigrant policies. The Program has three basic goals:

- To study the domestic and international issues raised by the 1986 Immigration Reform and Control Act (IRCA);

- To address the larger question and problems that continue to characterize immigration and immigrant policies;

- To disseminate and exchange information about IRCA, immigration and immigrant policies through publications, working groups, and conferences.

The Program publishes books and Immigration Policy Reports. The Program's research will help policymakers identify the degree to which IRCA is achieving its objectives. The research should also help practitioners assess the effectiveness of several previously untested "tools" of immigration policy.

Conclusions or opinions expressed are those of the authors and do not necessarily reflect the views of other staff members, officers, trustees, or advisory groups of either the RAND Corporation or The Urban Institute, or any organizations that provide either of them with financial support.

Persons interested in receiving the Program's publications or in attending its working groups and conferences should address enquiries to either of the Program's codirectors:

Dr. Frank D. Bean
The Urban Institute
2100 M Street, NW
Washington, DC 20037
(202) 833-7200

Dr. Georges Vernez
The RAND Corporation
1700 Main Street
Santa Monica, CA 90406
(213) 393-0411

SUMMARY AND OVERVIEW

In 1986 Congress addressed the issue of undocumented migration to the United States, enacting the Immigration Reform and Control Act (IRCA). The cornerstone of the law is a provision that for the first time makes it illegal for employers to hire undocumented immigrants. This employer sanctions provision is counterbalanced by a legislative ban on discrimination in employment on the basis of national origin or, under certain circumstances, citizenship status.

This completed study of the implementation of employer sanctions is part of a broader, two-year study of IRCA's implementation supported by the Ford Foundation and jointly conducted by The RAND Corporation and The Urban Institute.

We identify four major challenges to the implementers of the law, most notably the Immigration and Naturalization Service (INS): (1) establishing the legitimacy of sanctions as a new set of employment regulations; (2) satisfying the exacting legal requirements that attach to business regulation (and generally do not apply to relations with immigrants); (3) adapting the INS, which was designed for one purpose, to deal with individual immigrants, to the very different purposes of educating, regulating, inspecting, and sanctioning employers; and (4) regulating a vast economic process with limited investigative and enforcement resources. These challenges form the framework for evaluating IRCA's implementation.

Our assessment takes into account several basic historical characteristics of the lead implementing agency--the INS. Prior to IRCA, the Agency had little experience directly regulating U.S. employers. Furthermore, over the years its enforcement branches had been chronically undermanned, the Agency had grown highly decentralized, and it had historically been subject to criticism for the arbitrariness of its enforcement activity. All of these points raised concerns about the legitimacy and effectiveness of INS enforcement of IRCA.

We conclude that the implementers have essentially met the challenges of IRCA's first three years. The INS has averted significant complaints about unfair or overzealous employer sanctions enforcement. The Agency has generally stayed within the bounds of administrative law, which to a greater degree than immigration law emphasizes the rights of the regulated over the powers of the regulators, and the INS has avoided legal reversals that would cripple future implementation. The Agency has begun transforming itself from a paramilitary and police agency into a regulatory law enforcement agency that emphasizes investigative and educational activities. Local enforcement efforts have been reasonably well-designed to inform millions of employers about their obligations and to create incentives for compliance.

However, this progress is largely due to the decision to go slow on enforcement, a decision for which Congress itself deserves credit, as IRCA mandates employer education and a gradual transition to full enforcement.

Moreover, the question remains whether current implementation arrangements are a good foundation for the future. If implementation proceeds along current lines, will it continue meeting the challenges of legitimacy, legality, organizational adaptation, and effective use of enforcement resources? The answer is no. Arrangements that were adequate for the start-up phase would be seriously inadequate for a more mature program.

Several implementation issues threaten the future of employer sanctions:

- Inconsistencies in policy and tactics among different areas of the country and between Border Patrol and INS district office investigators could create serious inequities in the treatment of employers;

- A low level of enforcement activity could lead many employers to discount the possibility that violations will be detected and punished, thus weakening the deterrent effect of employer sanctions;

- A lack of clarity about the grounds on which the INS would seek criminal penalties could lead to crippling legal challenges;

- Failure to develop strong investigative capabilities will limit the INS's effectiveness in dealing with the most heavily immigrant-dependent employers. In many cities most immigrant-dependent firms are small, mobile, and in industries with low barriers to entry; enforcement can reach them only if investigators have good systems for tracking and monitoring the proprietors.

In the future, employer sanctions implementation needs to be strengthened in four ways:

- Central policy oversight must be strengthened to prevent unequal treatment of similarly situated employers in different parts of the country;

- The share of total Agency resources dedicated to sanctions enforcement needs to be sustained to ensure that investigations are thorough and that employers continue to believe that violations will be detected;

- Local enforcement should be coordinated to eliminate inconsistencies in targeting and enforcement criteria used by INS district offices and the Border Patrol;

- The use of random or "neutral" targeting strategies should be reaffirmed and strengthened to deflect charges of selective enforcement, and to monitor shifts in compliance across industries and geographic regions.

The study's major findings are set out below.

FINDINGS

1.   In the eight sites in our sample, few civil or criminal fines had been assessed relative to the number of establishments covered or the number of investigators assigned to sanctions enforcement.

In Chicago, where the fewest fines were assessed, agents were issuing Notices of Intent to Fine at the rate of one for every two agent-years through the spring of 1989. For the most active local agency, the El Paso Border Patrol, the rate was one for every two staff months. This cannot be characterized as the overzealous enforcement that some feared prior to IRCA's enactment.

To some degree, this moderation is the logical result of legislative and administrative design. Congress intended that sanctions enforcement be phased in gradually, with full enforcement suspended until June 1988, and until November 1988 for agriculture. To this end, enforcement was to emphasize education rather than punishment--an emphasis that absorbed staff and resources. Also, INS officials intended enforcement to be circumspect in order to limit employer burden, avoid congressional sunset, and survive intense early scrutiny by GAO and others. Furthermore, low numbers of cases at the start are partly due to an effort in many local offices to ensure that early cases are strong ones based on what one INS attorney described as "terrific lead pipe evidence."

In other respects, low levels of penalties reflect constraints faced by the INS in implementing a new regulatory regime with extraordinarily broad coverage. Despite the fact that district Investigations staffs that shoulder the burden of enforcement were doubled following IRCA, they remained small and staffs were inexperienced. Low levels of penalties are also attributable to the fact that strong sanctions cases that allege the knowing hiring of undocumented workers can be hard to make given the affirmative defense that the law affords employers who have completed I-9s on their workers.

Finally, INS had to deal with complicated evasion techniques. These include the obvious enforcement problems presented by the easy availability of false documents, a problem complicated by the array of probable and improbable work documents that have been issued by the INS over time.

2.   The enforcement of IRCA's sanctions provisions
     varied sharply in terms of priorities, processes,
     targets, and fines.

Priorities. Local INS enforcement officials have to respond
to a myriad of law enforcement missions assigned the
Agency over the course of the past five years, including
drug enforcement, the removal of criminal aliens from U.S.
prisons, enforcement of the 1986 Immigration Marriage
Fraud Amendments and, in some sites, investigation and
prosecution of fraud in the Special Agricultural Worker
(SAW) legalization program under IRCA.

SITE ENFORCEMENT PRIORITIES

Site	Priority
New York	Criminal alien
El Paso	Alien apprehension
Houston	SAWs fraud
Miami	Criminal alien
San Antonio	Criminal alien
Chicago	Employer sanctions
Los Angeles	Employer sanctions

Sanctions was the highest priority within our sites only
in Chicago and Los Angeles. In New York, Miami, and
San Antonio, drugs and criminal aliens dominated the
enforcement agenda. In Houston, sanctions enforcement
had been largely eclipsed by the district office's prosecution of fraud in the SAW program.

Processes. In some sites local INS offices had adopted a
"regulatory" style of sanctions enforcement. This approach

emphasizes employer education and the development of cases on the basis of document analysis. Investigations are multistage in character and start with an education visit, are followed by a three-day notice of inspection, an I-9 inspection, the transmittal of a notice of results letter, a follow-up inspection, and only then a "survey" or a raid. In some instances this survey is scheduled at the employers' convenience. This regulatory enforcement model predominated in larger metropolitan areas, i.e., in New York, Chicago, and Los Angeles.

In other sites, the enforcement process could be characterized as following a more traditional "police" model. In these instances, a survey or raid is initiated early in the investigation/enforcement process. Undocumented aliens are apprehended and interviewed for evidence against their employer. Analysis of I-9s and other relevant documents occurs later, only when a probable violation is already established. This process was most in evidence in sites closer to the border.

Targets. The sites varied in whether employers or immigrants are the principal targets of enforcement. In some sites, the traditional INS mission of removing, capturing, and reporting undocumented aliens remained paramount. In other cities, the traditional goals were subordinated to the sanctions goal of discouraging employers from hiring unauthorized workers.

In Chicago, for example, INS investigators did not remove undocumented aliens from the workplace once they were detected. Rather, they were given voluntary departure, the employer was informed of their status, and both were made aware that follow-up inspections would take place. In other sites, however, INS used inspections of employer records as opportunities to apprehend aliens rather than change employers' practices.

Fines and fine policy. We observed two broad approaches to fine policy. One, typical of the Northern and

Eastern regions of the INS, involved issuing comparatively few but large, visible fines and the imposition of relatively few technical paperwork-only fines. The other approach, evident in Southern and Western regions, was to issue a comparatively large number of Notices of Intent to Fine (NIF), many of them for small face amounts, many citing only technical violations. These violations may reflect local political imperatives, personalities, or chance events. But they may also reflect strategic adaptation to differences in the size of the foreign-born population and its concentration within the regional economy.

AVERAGE FINES ASSESSED FOR VIOLATION

Site	No. NIFs	Average NIFs
Chicago	11	$45,545
New York	53	11,511
El Paso District	21	6,645
Miami	22	5,385
Los Angeles	67	4,458
Pembroke Pines BP (Miami)	53	3,975
El Paso BP	99	3,900
Houston	53	3,865
Laredo	48	2,892
San Antonio	57	850

Within our sites we found striking levels of variation in average fines assessed, ranging from $45,000 per NIF in Chicago to $850 in San Antonio.

Overall, INS penalties fall most heavily on small firms, many of which appear to be owned by ethnics. This pattern was less pronounced in New York, Chicago, and Los Angeles, where violations were cited within a relatively wide range of industries, many of them larger mainstream firms.

SHARE OF NIFS THAT DO NOT
SITE A KNOWING VIOLATION

Study Site	Percent Paper-Work Only
Los Angeles	51
El Paso	43
Pembroke Pines BP (Miami)	30
El Paso BP	23
New York	21
Laredo BP	15
San Antonio	12
Miami	5
Houston	2
Chicago	0

3. We did not observe extensive use of criminal sanctions under IRCA's pattern and practice and harboring and transporting provisions. Only half of our sites initiated any criminal enforcement actions.

This can be explained by the difficulty of making a case that meets the burden of proof needed to win criminal conviction. The investigative challenges proved too complicated for INS's inexperienced agents. Furthermore, the INS had little success getting U.S. attorneys to take and prosecute cases. Criminal cases are expensive to prosecute and by summer 1989 several local INS offices were running into budget problems.

4.   We observed limited coordination among IRCA's implementers. This was true both within the INS and between the INS and other implementers.

In a number of our sites sanctions were being enforced by both INS Investigations branches and the Border Patrol (BP). However, coordination between the two branches was weak. We found INS's Investigations and Border Patrol offices using different targeting, investigative, and penalty strategies in the same jurisdiction. Furthermore, we found that local INS offices rarely relied on leads provided by Department of Labor inspectors in targeting investigations.

As we noted above, U.S. attorneys' offices have yet to become fully enlisted in the effort to enforce IRCA's criminal sanctions provisions.

5.   Our interviews with the limited sample of employers in immigrant-dependent industries suggested that there is a high level of awareness of sanctions on the part of both large and small firms.

However, the completeness and accuracy of their compliance with the law's verification requirements--i.e., whether the employer asks for correct documents to verify work authorization--is a function of firm size, the existence of preestablished personnel procedures, and parallel contracting and regulatory requirements that require background checks for job applicants.

Chapter One

INTRODUCTION

In February 1988, the Ford Foundation provided a grant to establish a Program for Research on Immigration Policy at The RAND Corporation and The Urban Institute. The Program is intended to be a national resource for the study of immigration--the causes of immigration to the U.S., its effects on the U.S. and sending countries, immigrants' assimilation into the U.S. economy and society, and the effects of government policy on all aspects of the immigration process.

The Program's first major task was to study the early implementation of P.L. 99-603, The Immigration Reform and Control Act of 1986, commonly known as IRCA. That statute broke new ground in U.S. immigration policy in several ways--by making it illegal for U.S. employers to knowingly hire undocumented aliens; by creating opportunities for long-term illegal residents to gain legal status and apply for citizenship; by establishing a federal grant program to help state and local governments pay for services to newly legalized aliens; by offsetting agricultural employers' loss of immigrant labor by authorizing the legalization of former agricultural workers and by forbidding discrimination against authorized workers on the basis of national origin or, under certain circumstances, citizenship.

This research report, the result of a two-year collaboration between The Urban Institute and The RAND Corporation, analyzes the implementation of the key provisions of IRCA affecting employers. IRCA forbade employers to hire illegal aliens, and established a public information and regulatory apparatus both to help employers comply with the law and to detect and punish violations. IRCA also established an enforcement apparatus to ensure that employers comply with the laws banning discrimination in hiring on the basis of national origin or citizenship, and an appeal process to give persons who might have suffered discrimination a channel for redress.

The primary focus of this report is on actions taken by the federal government and private parties to implement and comply with IRCA's employer sanctions provisions. It analyzes those actions in light of the original expectations of IRCA's congressional and nongovernmental supporters, and explains how implementation was shaped by both local and national political and economic forces. Because implementation is an ongoing process, many important decisions remain to be made. We hope this report will help those who make and influence policy understand what has happened and why, and what choices remain.

IMPLEMENTATION RESEARCH

Implementation research focuses on events following the enactment of a law.[1] It is important because most decisions that affect a law's outcomes--whether it has the effects intended by its drafters and supporters and whether it creates unintended costs or benefits for different groups in society--are taken after a bill is passed and signed into law.[2] The distribution of powers in Congress ensures that appropriations decisions will be made by committees other than the ones that framed the law, and the separation of powers among the legislative, executive, and judicial branches ensures that most operational decisions about interpretation, timing, emphasis, and allocation of government manpower will be made outside Congress.[3] Major pieces of social legislation like IRCA stimulate actions by state and local governments, all of which face their own pressures and have distinct preferences and capabilities.[4] In IRCA's case, many key decisions must also be made by private parties-- employers, trade unions, voluntary service organizations, and attorneys.

The nature of the legislative process ensures that very important decisions will be left to the implementers. Congress seldom understands a phenomenon such as illegal immigration well enough to be comfortable prescribing detailed government actions. The law only establishes a broad framework within which implementers are to use their judgment and improve policy through trial and error. Legislative controversy also frequently leads to compromises on broad and inherently ambiguous verbal formulas that require subsequent interpretation. Bureaucrats and regulation writers often come under pressure from legislative factions that prefer particular interpretations, but the initiative belongs to the implementers.

Thus, implementation often determines what a law's outcomes will be. For those who might wish to change those outcomes or enhance the laws' effectiveness, understanding the implementation process is essential. Without such understanding, no one can attribute an unsatisfactory outcome to the law itself, to changeable aspects of the implementation process, or to the intractability of the problem being addressed. Without such understanding, no one can know whether a proposed reform is likely to have the desired effects.

This report examines the early implementation of IRCA's employer sanctions. It has four goals:

- To identify the problems employer sanctions posed for the INS, the organization primarily responsible for the implementation of sanctions;

- To document the implementers' general strategies for solving problems and to show how these strategies were translated into concrete action by decentralized regional and local federal agencies and by employers;

- To provide the first assessment of implementation performance to date; and

- To identify challenges that still must be met if employer sanctions are to have the effects intended by Congress.

RESEARCH STRATEGY

Our approach to studying the first three years of employer sanctions implementation has five key features:

Intent-based. We started by identifying the purposes the original sponsors hoped to achieve through employer sanctions and by tracing the compromises they had to make in order to gain enactment. This provided a set of assumptions about the problems employer sanctions were meant to solve, the law's impacts on the actions of local federal agencies and employers, and the distribution of its benefits and costs.

Longitudinal. Because policy was being made and refined throughout the time of the study and because different provisions took effect at different times, we made a series of observations rather than just one.

Multilevel. Though key implementation decisions were made in Washington, many were meant to be made at regional and local levels. Therefore, we studied both the transmission of national policy to the local level and the execution of policy by field agents and employers.

Multisite. Decentralization made it likely that policy and performance would differ from place to place. Local differences in economic structure, popular attitudes, and the size and composition of the immigrant population also made it likely that IRCA implementation would differ across sites. Therefore, we studied a number of localities selected to represent different areas of the country, political traditions, economic structure, and immigrant population size.

Cross-program. Though IRCA's many statutory provisions are legally separate, they are designed to interact. For example, the legalization program defines an alien population that employers can hire and retain without fear of sanctions; the antidiscrimination program constrains federal agencies' and employers' implementation of employer sanctions. Because IRCA's component programs can be fully understood only in relation to one another, we studied all IRCA programs in a locality simultaneously. Though this report will focus on employer sanctions, it will identify its key connections with other programs.

Between February 1988 and November 1989, we conducted interviews and collected data in Washington, D.C., the four regional offices of the INS, the state capitals of California, Texas, Florida, New York, and Illinois, and eight localities. The local sites were drawn from each of the four INS regions--San Jose and Los Angeles from the Western Region, New York from the Eastern Region, Chicago from the Northern Region, and San Antonio, El

Paso, Houston, and Miami from the Southern Region. All contain INS district offices, except San Jose, which houses a sub-office of the San Francisco District office. The INS Border Patrol was active at some level in four of the sites (Miami, Houston, San Antonio, and El Paso).

We visited each locality twice and conducted a standard set of interviews to permit assessment of differences among sites and of change over time within a site. Because Los Angeles is the destination of over 40 percent of all illegal immigrants and the locus of a corresponding share of the nation's policy development and advocacy activities, we maintained a continuous on-site monitoring project in that city.

Approximately 600 interviews were conducted over the duration of the study. Our principal respondents in Washington were congressional staff members, officials of the relevant domestic Cabinet departments, and interest group representatives. In regional INS offices, we interviewed the regional director, key associate directors, and leaders of the Border Patrol. Staffs of the governors, legislators, and major cabinet offices were our chief respondents in the state capitals. The majority of our interviews took place at the local level, with officials in the INS district office, union leaders, public service providers, church representatives, immigrant advocates and voluntary service organization leaders, political and civic leaders, and members of the immigration bar.

We also interviewed a total of 184 employers in our eight sites, exploring their role as both the targets and the enforcers of IRCA's employer requirements. (Under contract with the General Accounting Office, The Urban Institute has also conducted a study of hiring discrimination on the basis of national origin. That study's results will be reported separately.)

STUDY LIMITS

These data provide a rich and complex picture of IRCA implementation. However, our results are limited in four ways. First, because IRCA is still being implemented, final assessments are premature. Second, because our data collection focused on a small number of urban areas (though the ones with the vast majority of immigrants and employers likely to be strongly affected by IRCA), the results are not representative of all localities. In particular, they do not reflect impacts on agricultural employers or regions.

Third, we confronted substantial data constraints. We are aware of no national data set that effectively disaggregates to the INS sector or the district office level detailed, uniform information on the type of individual enforcement actions initiated (e.g., paperwork vs. knowing violations), proposed fine amounts, and eventual case disposition. Our best data source, which provides some of this detail, was discontinued in April 1989.

Fourth, we are able to analyze the chains of administrative and legal actions initiated by employer sanctions, but we cannot report on their ultimate effects on the lives of employers, workers, job applicants, or undocumented immigrants who were not eligible for legalization. In some cases we can anticipate effects based on the implementation patterns we have observed, but other research efforts conducted under the auspices of the Program for Research and Immigration Policy are meant to make such outcome assessments. This study is not.

Subsequent sections of this report cover the legislative background of employer sanctions and Congress's expectations for implementation; the challenges faced by IRCA's implementers and the policies adopted to meet the challenges; and implementation of employer sanctions at the local level by federal agencies and employers. We conclude with an assessment of implementation to date, and of new challenges that must be met in the near future.

Notes, chapter one

1. For a survey of recent implementation research, see Dennis J. Palumbo and Donald J. Calista (eds.), Symposium: Implementation: What We Have Learned and Still Need to Know, *Policy Studies Review*, Vol. 7, No. 1, Autumn 1987, pp. 91-246.

2. For elaboration see, for example, E. Hargrove, *The Missing Link*, Washington, D.C., The Urban Institute, 1975; R. T. Nakamura, The Textbook Policy Process and Implementation Research, *Policy Studies Review*, Autumn 1987, pp. 142-54. Also, see M. Rein and F. Rabinowitz, Implementation, a Theoretical Perspective, in W. D. Burnham and M. Weinberg (eds.), *American Politics and Public Policy*, Cambridge, MIT Press, 1978, pp. 307-355.

3. See R. Nakamura and F. Smallwood, *The Politics of Policy Implementation*, New York, St. Martins, 1980; and D. A. Mazmanian and P. A. Sabatier, *Implementation and Public Policy*, Glenview, Ill., Scott, Foresman, 1983.

4. For an analysis of the special problems in a federal system see, for example, L. McDonnell and R. Elmore, *Getting the Job Done: Alternative Policy Instruments, Educational Evaluation and Policy Analysis*, 9(2), 1987, 133-152; and C. Van Horn and D. S. Van Meter, "The Implementation of Intergovernmental Policy," in S. Nagel (ed.), *Policy Studies Review Annual*, Vol. 1, No. 1, Beverly Hills, Calif., Sage Publications, 1977.

Chapter Two

LEGISLATIVE BACKGROUND AND CONGRESSIONAL EXPECTATIONS

At the time of a law's enactment, the initiative shifts from Congress to the Executive branch. The Executive branch can write regulations, assign administrative responsibility, request necessary funding, resolve ambiguities in the legislation and settle disputes, and communicate policy to other levels of government or private actors affected by it. But implementation never emerges completely from the shadow of the legislative process. It is always influenced by the motives and hopes of its originators, the compromises they had to make in order to obtain a majority vote in Congress, the issues they left unresolved, and the opportunities they created for their own continued influence.

Most major pieces of social legislation are initiated or heavily influenced by the President and the Executive branch. IRCA was the result of wide-ranging political consultations, but it was, to an unusual degree, a congressional initiative. Though all administrations over the past two decades submitted a legislative package dealing with illegal immigration, the bills that received detailed scrutiny and markup were all drafted by leaders of the House and Senate Judiciary Committees. These leaders also managed the key negotiations with other committees, government agencies, and interest groups. Because Congress was so dominant in the development of

IRCA, the expectations of its congressional promoters--and the agreements they made in the course of legislative bargaining--set the agenda for implementation. In this chapter, we show how Congress's efforts to curb illegal immigration derive from and complement other legislative initiatives in the area of immigration policy. We proceed to sketch the arguments advanced for and against the adoption of employer sanctions during the Congress's 30 year debate over the issue. We then briefly describe IRCA's major provisions, focusing on those that most directly affect employers (i.e., sanctions and antidiscrimination), and conclude with a discussion of what Congress expected of sanctions' implementation and of IRCA's near-term outcomes. It is these expectations that we will use as a measure in assessing implementation to date. We should note that we have not attempted to duplicate here the several extensive legislative histories that have been written of IRCA.[1]

THE LEGISLATIVE CONTEXT FOR SANCTIONS

Over the last quarter century, Congress separately addressed the issues of legal immigration, refugee and asylum policy and, with IRCA, illegal immigration.[2] In general it could be argued that Congress's efforts in the two decades before IRCA effectively liberalized U.S. policy, making it more open to new immigration. IRCA, which embodied both inclusionary and exclusionary impulses, signaled the arrival of a more eclectic and somewhat less liberal period in congressional policy-making. These more conservative political inclinations are reflected by the restrictive Immigration Marriage Fraud

Amendments of 1986,[3] enacted four days after IRCA, and by proposals to cap annual immigrant admissions.[4] All have proposed to move immigration policy toward more stringent and deliberate regulation of entry into the country.

Congress's efforts to liberalize U.S. immigration law began in 1965 when it overturned the country-based quota system that had been established during the 1920s.[5] These quotas were the product of the restrictionist sentiments of the time and built in a bias toward admitting Northern and Western Europeans. The new admissions system was based on encouraging family unification and allowing persons with special skills to fill shortages in specific occupations. The effect of these ethnically neutral policies was to permit increased legal immigration from Southern Europe, Central and South America, and Asia.[6]

Following the fall of Vietnam and the appearance of a large refugee population in Southeast Asia, Congress again liberalized the immigration laws by enacting the 1980 Refugee Act.[7] The law removed ideological and geographic considerations from the definition of refugee, adopting the United Nations' more liberal standard of persons outside their native countries who are unable to return because of a "well founded fear of persecution."[8] The law also recognized for the first time the principle of asylum in U.S. immigration law[9] and was described during floor debate by then Congressman Peter Rodino (D.-N.J.) as "one of the most important pieces of humanitarian legislation ever enacted by a U.S. Congress."[10]

THE CASE FOR SANCTIONS

While both these laws made basic changes in U.S. immigration policy, neither addressed illegal immigration--an issue that was growing increasingly salient as apprehensions of illegal aliens mounted and as large numbers of Cuban and Haitian boat people arrived in Florida.

Debate over illegal immigration and the need for effective policies to counteract it had been a legislative perennial since Senator Paul Douglas of Illinois had first proposed sanctions legislation in the early 1950s.[11] In the 30 years between Douglas's first proposal and IRCA's final enactment, a complex set of economic and social arguments, both for and against sanctions, emerged. We sketch below some of the most influential and commonly encountered complaints about illegal immigration.

Sovereignty

One argument consistently made in favor of sanctions was that it would respond to the challenge that unregulated illegal immigration posed to the nation's sovereignty. The press's extensive reporting of alien apprehension statistics brought home forcefully this "failure to control our borders." With little change in INS enforcement resources, apprehensions had risen from 139,000 in 1966 to 1.3 million in 1985, and were expected to reach 1.8 million in 1986.

Former Attorney General Edwin Meese was a typical exponent of this position:

> Regaining control of our borders is an essential goal of any true immigration reform. We cannot fairly speak of ourselves as a sovereign nation if

we cannot responsibly decide who may cross our borders.[12]

The rhetoric of sovereignty had a darker side. Senator Jesse Helms (R.-N.C.) advanced a particularly dire view of the implications of illegal immigration for the nation's sovereignty that went beyond respect for law to a loss of territorial control. He cited comments by the Mexican writer Carlos Loret de Mola that "the Southwest seems to be slowly returning to the jurisdiction of Mexico without firing a single shot, nor requiring the least diplomatic action, by means of a steady, spontaneous, and uninterrupted occupation."[13]

Uncontrolled immigration also led centrists to examine the long-term political effects of sovereignty issues. For example, Father Theodore Hesburgh, chairman of the Select Commission on Immigration and Refugee Policy (SCIRP), worried that uncontrolled illegal immigration eliminated the United States' freedom of action in admitting legal immigrants. Such concerns over a backlash against legal immigration were frequently invoked throughout the legislative debate over IRCA.

Legal Symmetry

A second imperative for sanctions and for IRCA was an attempt to correct a long-standing asymmetry in American immigration law. While historically it had been illegal for undocumented immigrants to enter and work in the United States, it was not a violation of federal law to employ illegal aliens. This, in turn, made enforcement of the immigration laws needlessly difficult. As former Governor of Colorado Richard Lamm has written:

> Closing this loophole with the Simpson-Mazzoli
> bill or a similar bill would let the INS concen-
> trate its enforcement efforts on the few large-
> scale employers who openly flout immigration
> laws. By making the employers responsible, the
> INS could use its resources more effectively.
> Today, the INS is trying to locate illegals within
> the United States one by one, and it is unable to
> move against employers who openly hire them.
> This situation is analogous to trying to stop
> gambling by allowing bookies to operate openly
> and legally while attempting to locate individual
> bettors. It makes no sense and it is unfair.[14]

This asymmetry also meant that the nation's large
undocumented population lived without the protection of
the country's laws and were potentially subject to
exploitation and intimidation by unethical employers.

Jobs and Wages

From the outset of the discussions on sanctions, some
contended that undocumented immigrants took jobs from
Americans, particularly from low-income, unskilled
minorities. It was argued that illegal immigrants de-
pressed wages and that their presence led to a decline in
working conditions in the industries that employ them.
The Report of the Senate Judiciary Committee on the 1985
Immigration Reform and Control Act summarizes these
concerns:

> . . . we believe there have been adverse job
> impacts, especially on low-income, low-skilled
> Americans, who are the most likely to face direct
> competition, even though we also perceive a

degree of short term economic advantage from the use of "cheap" labor. Such adverse impacts include both unemployment and less favorable wages and working conditions. Not only does this cause economic harm to the directly affected Americans and their families, and in many cases a burden on the taxpayers, but it may also affect society as a whole in the form of social problems associated with unemployment and poverty.[15]

Social and Cultural Effects

Sanctions and IRCA were also driven by the presumed social and cultural effects of large-scale immigration--legal and illegal--from Mexico, Central America, the Caribbean and Asia. Concerns were raised about the institutionalization of foreign languages, the emergence of self-sufficient ethnic enclaves, the fragmentation of national and local communities and resulting ethnic tensions. The Senate Judiciary Report accompanying the 1985 Immigration Reform and Control Act again offers a relevant commentary:

> If immigration is continued at a high level, yet a substantial portion of these new persons and their descendants do not assimilate into the society, they have the potential to create in America a measure of the same social, political and economic problems which exist in the countries from which they have chosen to depart. Furthermore, if language and cultural separatism rise above a certain level, the unity and political stability of the Nation will--in time--be seriously diminished.[16]

Natural Resources

One set of advocates for sanctions emerged from the environmental and zero-population growth movements. They viewed the threat of massive illegal immigration as extending to natural resources and the environment. A persuasive spokesman for this point of view was former Colorado Governor Richard Lamm, who has written: "People pollute, and too many people living in an area can degrade that area irrevocably. Immigration at high levels exacerbates our resource and environmental problems. It will leave a poorer, more crowded, more divided country for our children."[17]

Public Benefits

It was frequently contended that immigrants to the country were drawn not just by the lure of jobs, but by the U.S.'s generous public benefit programs. Indeed Congress's impression that unauthorized aliens were drawing public benefits led to the inclusion of the Systematic Alien Verification for Entitlement Program (SAVE) within IRCA. SAVE requires that state and local welfare officials verify the citizenship of applicants for AFDC, Medicaid, unemployment compensation, food stamps, housing assistance and higher education programs.

These fiscal concerns were aggravated by the Supreme Court's 1982 ruling in *Plyler v. Doe,*[18] which held that local school districts had a constitutional obligation to provide education to all children, regardless of their immigration status. The political force of the public benefits issue, like so many others associated with efforts to curb illegal immigration, was tied to the fact that immigration is a localized phenomenon that has a disproportionate effect on a few states and localities. Not surprisingly, these jurisdictions began to take an intense interest in trying to influence those elements of federal immigration policy that had a direct impact on their tax revenues.

Again, competition for scarce public resources underlay arguments for immigration reform. Richard Lamm cast these issues in their broadest context during testimony before the Congressional Joint Economic Committee. He stated:

> The United States already faces a staggering social agenda. We have not adequately integrated blacks into our economy or our society. We have an education system rightly described as a "rising tide of mediocrity." Fifty percent of our Hispanic students never graduate from high school; we have the most violent society of the industrialized world; we have startlingly high rates of illiteracy, illegitimacy, and welfare. It takes an incredible hubris to madly rush, with these unfinished agendas, into blindly accepting more immigrants and refugees than all of the rest of the world put together, and still hope that we can keep a common agenda.[19]

OPPOSITION TO SANCTIONS

But sanctions had a set of staunch, politically powerful opponents that included the agricultural industry, a coalition of civil rights and immigrant advocacy organizations, as well as civil libertarians. They argued the case against sanctions on several grounds.

Dependence on Undocumented Labor

Some industries--most notably agriculture--were frank about their dependence on undocumented labor and the severe financial problems that sanctions would impose. Some even contended that employers would be unable to find alternative sources of labor and would have no alternative but to disobey the law. An editorial in the *Wall Street Journal*, a long-time foe of sanctions, argued that:

> The result [of IRCA] is employers turning farms and restaurants into work-easies, running afoul of the law by hiring aliens for jobs no one else will do. Legislation in the face of such over-whelming demand in the marketplace is surely doomed to failure. How much moralizing and how many arrests must we endure in this second period of prohibition?[20]

Furthermore, broad political support for sanctions was eroded by claims that undocumented workers took jobs that native workers would shun, thereby keeping low-wage manufacturing jobs and industries in the U.S. and stimulating local economies. All told, this meant that undocumented immigrants did not appear to reduce the job opportunities available to disadvantaged native minorities.[21]

Discrimination

The argument against sanctions that had the greatest political force was advanced by civil rights organizations and ethnic advocacy groups. They contended that the imposition of civil and criminal liability on employers for hiring undocumented workers would lead employers to avoid hiring any foreign-sounding and foreign-looking workers. Vilma Martinez of the Mexican American Legal Defense and Education Fund stated:

> For Mexican Americans and other Americans who share the physical characteristics of persons thought to be undocumented, employer sanctions will exacerbate existing patterns of employment discrimination. Well-meaning employers, fearful of Government sanctions, will shy away from hiring us. Racist or biased employers will simply use the fear of sanctions as an excuse to avoid hiring us. At the very least, employers untrained in intricate immigration laws are likely to err in their assessment of who is undocumented.[22]

Compliance Burden

While the mainstream of U.S. business and commerce was reluctant to admit to a dependence on undocumented workers, its spokesmen, particularly the U.S. Chamber of Commerce, argued that sanctions' verification requirements would prove a burden on business. Opposition intensified following the defeat of proposals that would have limited IRCA's verification requirements to (a) firms found violating the law's ban on hiring undocumented workers, and (b) firms with more than four employees.

Privacy

Representatives of civil liberties organizations, especially the American Civil Liberties Union, complained that the success of sanctions would eventually depend on creation of some form of national identification card. The card, along with the national databases that might be needed to enable employers to determine job applicants' work eligibility, represented steps on a "slippery slope" to the erosion of constitutional safeguards for individual privacy.

As we shall see in the next section, each of these arguments had a powerful impact on shaping IRCA and its sanctions provisions.

IRCA'S MAIN PROVISIONS

By the time of its enactment, IRCA had become an omnibus law, as sanctions had been packaged with at least six other major provisions. Each represented a political trade that had been added as a way of regulating or mitigating the consequences, first of employer sanctions, and later of one another. They include:

- an expansion of existing civil rights laws, barring discrimination in hiring on the basis of national origin or, under certain circumstances, citizenship status;

- a legalization program for individuals who had resided continuously in the U.S. since January 1, 1982;

- a legalization program for individuals who had worked for 90 days or more in agriculture in any of the three years preceding IRCA's enactment (the Special Agricultural Worker program, or SAW); as well as a subsequent legalization program for Replenishment Agricultural

Workers (RAW). The number of persons who might be admitted as RAWs would be contingent upon the number of SAWs leaving agricultural employment and the adequacy of the supply of labor available to growers of perishable commodities during fiscal years 1990-1993;

- a four billion dollar intergovernmental grants program intended to help state and local governments offset the impact of legalization (the State Legalization Impact Assistance Grant program, or SLIAG);

- mandatory national adoption of a database and computer-matching program to verify that applicants for certain public benefit programs are citizens or are otherwise eligible for their receipt (the Systematic Alien Verification for Entitlement program, or SAVE).

- expansion of a program to deport aliens convicted of crimes.

While employer sanctions remained the keystone of the law, the concerns of sanctions' opponents, described below, found their way into IRCA's overall structure, driving the inclusion of many of the main provisions cited above:

- Concerns on the part of Hispanic and other civil rights organizations led to inclusion of the legalization program to avoid the mass deportation of millions of undocumented migrants living in the United States at the time of the law's enactment. The program was supported by employers who viewed legalization as one means of satisfying their labor supply needs in a post-IRCA environment.

- Civil rights groups' concerns about the potential of sanctions to lead to increased discrimination against lawful job applicants of foreign, especially Latin American, origin led to the enactment of the antidiscrimination provisions as well as provisions making possible the repeal of sanctions should they result in "widespread discrimination."

- Growers' concerns about their future labor supply were met by the extraordinarily liberal, one-time Special Agricultural Worker program (SAW) and by a Replenishment Agricultural Worker program (RAW) that would continue to legalize potential farm workers should SAWs abandon agricultural employment and should the need for labor persist.

IRCA's employer requirements themselves embodied the trade-offs and compromises made between sanctions' opponents and advocates, as the discussion below indicates.

Employer Sanctions

The employer sanctions provisions of IRCA prohibit three types of activity: (1) the knowing hiring of unauthorized aliens; (2) the continued employment of known unauthorized aliens; and (3) the hiring of any individual without verifying identity and authorization to work (the law's "paperwork" requirements). The law requires that all employers verify the authorization to work of employees hired after November 6, 1986, and maintain records (i.e., I-9s) indicating that the employee's eligibility was verified. In so doing, the Congress sought to impress the vast private administrative apparatus of the nation's employers into service. The strategy was intended to substantially expand the enforcement capacity of the government without incurring immense costs.

Sanctions represents the announcement of a broad, tough, new regulatory regime. This is reflected in the breadth of the law's coverage, as it extends not only to the nation's seven million firms, but to the employment transactions of individuals.[23] Moreover, the provisions are not limited to full-time employees, but to all situations where an employer/employee relationship has been entered into.[24] Furthermore, to close a loophole that has reduced the effectiveness of similar schemes in some European countries, IRCA expressly makes general contractors equally liable with subcontractors for the knowing hiring of unauthorized aliens.[25]

The law requires that applicants for employment attest to the fact that they are authorized to work by signing an "I-9" form. It requires that employers also sign the form, pledging under penalty of perjury that they have examined specified documents to determine the applicants' identity and work eligibility. The burden on employers and applicants imposed by these verification requirements is mitigated somewhat by the fact that many different documents are deemed acceptable to establish work eligibility and by the fact that employers are required to accept a proferred document if it "reasonably appears on its face to be genuine."[26] At the same time, however, the law makes it a separate offense, punishable by a fine, for an employer to refuse to produce I-9 forms upon the request of an INS or Department of Labor inspector, whether or not those officials have obtained a warrant.[27]

The scope of employers' new liability and the real power of sanctions are best revealed by the law's penalty provisions. IRCA sets out a graduated set of penalties for the knowing hiring of unauthorized workers of $250 to $2000 per worker for the first violation; $2000 to $5000 per worker for the second violation; and $3000 to $10,000 for the third and subsequent violations. The law also authorizes the INS to issue a cease-and-desist order. Violation of the paperwork requirements can result in fines of $100 to $1000. Unlike violations of the knowing or continuing-to-hire requirements, the penalty for paperwork violations is not graduated, that is, the range remains the same, regardless of the number of violations.

Significantly, the law also provides for criminal penalties for violators of the employer sanctions provisions who engage in a "pattern or practice" of knowing hires of unauthorized aliens. The statute does not define what constitutes a pattern or practice, but the legislative history indicates that the term applies to "regular, repeated and intentional activities but does not include sporadic or accidental acts." The prosecution of a pattern or practice violation does not seem to depend on serial, preexisting convictions for violating the law's sanctions provisions. That is, an employer can be charged with a "pattern and practice" violation despite the fact that he has not previously been fined under IRCA's employer requirements.

The law contains a second criminal provision, which states that it is a felony to transport anyone into or within the U.S. with the intention of concealing, harboring, or shielding them from detection in the U.S.[28] Prior to IRCA's enactment, the impact of these harboring and transporting provisions was mitigated by the "Texas Proviso," which specifically stated that employment and the "incidents of employment" did not constitute harboring. In practice, the graduated system of civil fines and the pattern and practice provisions of IRCA will mean that the mere knowing or continuing to hire of an unauthorized alien will rarely be prosecuted as a felony. However, employers who transport or conceal undocumented aliens can be subject to felony prosecutions.

While the breadth of the law's coverage and the potential severity of its penalties cannot be denied, concessions to sanctions' opponents that limit the burden and liabilities it imposes can also be seen in the way the provision was eventually framed.

First, the imposition of heavy penalties that would cumulate with each separate infraction are reserved for "knowing" violations of the law.[29] While "paperwork only" (or technical violations) were contemplated, their dollar value is comparatively low and repeated violations do not lead to escalating fines or to eventual criminal action.[30] The knowledge requirement, coupled with the directive that employers are only responsible for determining if documents are reasonable on their face, restricts employers' liability and limits their compliance burden while at the same time reducing their incentive to discriminate against foreign-sounding and foreign-looking job applicants.

Another concession to opponents was that sanctions were to be phased in gradually. No enforcement was authorized from the date of enactment through June 1, 1987,[31] and the following calendar year, June 1 to May 31, 1988, was designated as a "citation period."[32] During this year the INS was only to issue a citation for an initial violation. After being cited for a first offense, an employer could be fined for subsequent offenses committed during the period. In short, offenders during this year-long citation period got "one bite at the apple."

INS activities during these two periods were primarily informational in character, as the Agency sought to inform employers about their new responsibilities under the law. Full enforcement of the law for all industries other than agriculture began on June 1, 1988. At that time, all detected violations were subject to fine. Full enforcement in agriculture did not begin until December 1, 1988.[33]

To mitigate sanctions' adverse effects on the supply of labor, employers were relieved of any obligation to verify the citizenship status of employees hired before IRCA's enactment on November 6, 1986, and who had worked without interruption for the same employer since that time.[34] However, IRCA does not confer any legal status on these undocumented "grandfathered" workers, who are deportable if they are apprehended.

To appease agricultural employers, the law required for the first time that INS officers have a warrant or consent before they could search a farm or outdoor agricultural operation.[35] (No other provision of IRCA, with the possible exception of the Special Agricultural Worker program was as strongly opposed by the INS during congressional deliberations as this new warrant requirement.)

Finally, the law provided for intensive scrutiny by the General Accounting Office of sanctions' impact to determine, among other things, whether they would lead to "widespread discrimination." Such a finding on the part of the GAO would lead to expedited congressional review and, possibly, the "sunset" of the sanctions provisions. This would occur after the submission of the GAO's annual report following the third full year of the law's implementation.[36]

NONDISCRIMINATION

From an employer's perspective, IRCA may represent not one but two new regimes of regulation. The law represents a modest expansion in the coverage of U.S. civil rights law to reach discrimination in employment arising in the wake of IRCA's enactment. IRCA makes it unlawful for an employer to discriminate against someone eligible to work in the U.S. on the basis of (a) national origin or (b) citizenship status if he or she is a citizen or what is termed an "intending" citizen (except that U.S. citizens may be preferred if they are "equally qualified"). The law creates a new office within the Department of Justice, the Office of Special Counsel for Immigration-Related Unfair Employment Practices, to investigate and pursue charges of discrimination.[37]

The law is intended to complement civil rights protections announced in Title VII of the 1964 Civil Rights Act. It does so in two ways. First, it extends the existing ban on discrimination on the basis of national origin to firms with from 4 to 14 employees (Title VII applies only to firms with more than 15 employees). Second, the law announces for the first time a ban on discrimination in employment on the basis of alienage or citizenship status.

While the provision itself represents something of a victory for civil rights organizations and immigrant advocacy groups, the Congress mitigated its impact on employers in a number of ways. First, the law's coverage is limited to permanent resident aliens, temporary resident aliens, refugees, and asylees who declare themselves to be "intending citizens."[38] Second, unlike Title VII, it is restricted to hiring and terminations--and does not reach the "terms and conditions" of employment.[39] Third, the law vests only a limited right of private action in those who believe they have been victims of discrimination. Complaints must be filed with the Office of Special Counsel (or the Equal Employment Opportunity Commission).[40] Only if the government decides not to pursue the case can the individual sue the employer directly.[41] Fourth, the law permits employers to select citizens over non-citizens where both are "equally qualified."[42] Finally, unlike IRCA's sanctions provisions, the law exempts employers with fewer than four employees.[43]

CONGRESSIONAL EXPECTATIONS AND "IMPLEMENTATION CONSTRAINTS"

The leaders of the House and Senate Judiciary Committees, Democratic Representatives Romano Mazzoli and Peter Rodino and Republican Senator Alan Simpson, consistently pressed for enactment and managed negotiations with key congressional and executive branch factions. Despite the bipartisan collaboration among its originators, however, IRCA was controversial in Congress. Precursor bills were enacted by either the House or Senate (but not both) in the 95th, 96th, and 97th Congresses, and only a conference committee impasse prevented enactment in the 98th Congress. Most observers of the 99th Congress expected IRCA to die in conference again but were surprised when a last minute compromise on legalization of special agricultural workers made agreement possible.

IRCA reserves for Congress an important place in the implementation process. Scheduled reports from the GAO and the president give Congress information and the opportunity to conduct substantive oversight hearings. The prospect of sunset gives opponents (or disillusioned supporters) of employer sanctions a specific opportunity to marshal their objections. It also ensures that implementing agencies and the staunch congressional supporters of employer sanctions will be alert to the expectations and concerns of those members of Congress who might provide "swing" votes on a sunset initiative.

Understanding that these concerns about sanctions' implementation and impacts were likely to constrain IRCA's implementation, we decided to take explicit account of them in our analysis. We conducted in-depth interviews with members of Congress and senior staff members who were involved in the drafting of key IRCA provisions and in the amendment of the original employer sanctions proposals. We also reviewed written accounts by the same sources. Through these interviews, we assessed the personal and unofficial expectations of IRCA's framers and supporters. They are, in effect, the political signals emanating from Congress, rather than the official "legislative intent," which is defined by legal scholarship and judicial interpretation.

We analyzed the interview results to find general themes that cut across partisan differences, and extracted the following:

> *The original House and Senate Judiciary Committee drafters of IRCA were most concerned about establishing the principle that employers could not legally hire undocumented immigrants.*

They thought the internal consistency of our legal system required establishment of such a principle, regardless of whether it was financially, technically, or politically possible to enforce it rigorously in the short run. As Alan Simpson said in introducing IRCA to the Senate in 1985: ". . . The most basic function of a sovereign nation . . . is to control the entry of aliens across its borders and to enforce whatever conditions are imposed on the aliens who we so allow to enter . . . "

But as senior Senate aide Richard Day later explained, "Senator Simpson and Congressman Mazzoli began with an understanding that illegal immigration was a phenomenon that had to be dealt with, not a problem which could be solved."[45]

> *The originators expected the principle itself to have some effect on employers' practices, but they recognized that industries that depended heavily on illegal aliens would not change overnight.*

Though they would not be satisfied if the principle were rendered utterly moot in practice, they did not expect sudden complete enforcement or compliance. Some said that a 75 percent compliance rate among employers was acceptable in the first few years after enactment. ". . . [N]obody ever thought it [sanctions] would stop illegal migration into the United States. But we thought it would reduce it, and there was no way to have any kind of rational and reasonable border control without having a law that prohibited employers from knowingly hiring the people that slipped by the Border Patrol . . . . We know the European experience. It took them years to develop a degree of effectiveness."[46]

> *The originators were concerned from the beginning about the costs that the employer requirements would impose on business, and the need to soften business opposition heightened their concern.*

They were also alert to the INS's poor reputation in the business community. The "grandfather" clause permitting employers to retain long-term illegal employees and the law's emphasis on employer education and phased-in enforcement reflect sympathy with employers who had come to rely on a legally acceptable alien work force. The INS was specifically required to conduct community outreach and help employers find alternative labor supplies.

The originators and the congressional allies of business groups whose support was necessary for passage of IRCA did not want sanctions to create local labor shortages or cause abrupt wholesale turnovers of employers' labor forces.

The legalization, SAW, RAW, and expedited H-2 programs (which provided for accelerated processing of work visas for selected immigrant agricultural workers) were Congress's primary efforts to guarantee a good supply of labor. As Richard Day, counsel to the Senate Immigration Subcommittee, explained, "It [IRCA] should not cause any great disruption in the labor market. There was no intent to have mass deportations or even mass departures . . . The Immigration and Naturalization Service can best use its resources preventing new . . . illegal entries at the border rather than in trying to ferret out long-term illegal residents in the United States. And he [Simpson] frequently said, "I do not want to be part of a country that is on the hunt for people."

The framers hoped the Office of Management and Budget and the appropriations committees would support increased inspections efforts, but they did not aspire to levels of funding that would provide more than fractional coverage of the nation's employers. Though senior Judiciary Committee members were willing to press for larger INS appropriations, they recognized that their leverage was limited during times of severe fiscal constraints, and they acknowledged that enforcement would be a relatively small-scale effort for the foreseeable future. Early in the implementation process, senior members of the Judiciary Committee staff acknowledged, "We got caught just as we passed this bill intending to beef up enforcement with the budget deficit problem, and INS has had to take its lumps just like everybody else."[47]

> *IRCA's originators and supporters were willing to contemplate punitive actions against employers found deliberately employing illegal aliens. They did not expect enforcers to seek criminal sanctions except in cases where employers were recalcitrant or deceptive.*

In such cases, however, congressional supporters assumed that violators could generate little political sympathy and could, therefore, safely be penalized severely. Congress authorized much more lenient penalties for paperwork-only violations and insisted that more serious fines be assessed only against employers who knowingly and persistently employed illegal aliens.

These points are important because they set constraints on implementation. Based only on the foregoing, we could anticipate that implementation would be:

- nonconfrontational, based on an opening assumption that most employers are law abiding;

- staged, seeking compliance as a first priority and punishment only as a signal to others or as a last resort against stubborn violators;

- modestly funded and thus small in scale relative to the number of potential objects of enforcement;

- sensitive to local labor force conditions and the needs of individual firms;

- careful to avoid charges of harassment on technicalities.

In the following chapter we examine the degree to which those objectives were realized in practice.

Notes, chapter two

1. See, for example, U.S. House of Representatives, Committee on the Judiciary, Immigration Control and Legalization Amendments Act of 1986, Report 99-682, Washington D.C., 1986; U.S. Senate, Committee on the Judiciary, Immigration Reform and Control Act of 1985, Report 99-132, Washington D.C., 1985; Nancy Humel Montweiler, *The Immigration Reform Law of 1986: Analysis, Text, Legislative History,* The Bureau of National Affairs, Washington D.C., 1987; Joyce C. Vialet, *Immigration Issues and Legislation in the 99th Congress,* Congressional Research Service, Washington, D.C., 1986; Alan K. Simpson, U.S. Immigration Reform: Employer Sanctions and Antidiscrimination Provisions, *University of Arkansas at Little Rock Law Review,* Vol. 9, No. 4, 1986-1987; and Maurice A. Roberts and Stephen Yale-Lohr, *Understanding the 1986 Immigration Law,* Federal Publications, Washington D.C., 1988.

2. Indeed, it now appears that the cycle has come full circle as the Congress is now intensively debating substantial reform of legal immigration policy. See S. 358, 101st Congress, 1st Sess. Cong. Record (135) (daily ed., July 14, 1989).

3. P.L. 99-639, 100 Stat. 3537. The Immigration Marriage Fraud Amendments (IMFA) provide, among other things, that certain spouses and sons and daughters who become permanent resident aliens by virtue of marriage will remain in conditional

status for two years. IMFA also increased the criminal penalty for marriage fraud.

4. S.358. The Immigration Act of 1989. Cong. Record 96 (daily ed., July 14, 1990).

5. The Immigration and Nationality Act Amendments of 1965, P.L. 89-236; 79 Stat. 911.

6. See Harris Miller, 'The Right Thing to Do': A History of Simpson-Mazzoli, *Journal of Contemporary Studies*, Fall 1984.

7. P.L. 96-212.

8. Refugee Act of 1980, Sec. 201.

9. Frank Bean, Georges Vernez, and Charles Keely, *Opening and Closing the Doors*, Program for Research on Immigration Policy, The RAND Corporation and The Urban Institute, Washington, D.C., Urban Institute Press, 1989; p. 92.

10. Cong. Record (126) (daily ed., March 4, 1980).

11. Lawrence H. Fuchs, The Blood of All Nations: The Triumph of Inclusivity in Immigration Policy, in *Ethnicity and Public Policy* (forthcoming, 1990).

12. 1985 Immigration Subcommittee hearings on H.R. 3080, Serial No. 28, p. 4, cited at H. Rept 99-682, Pt 1, Immigration Legalization Amendments of 1986, House Judiciary Committee, 99th Cong. 2nd Sess. 1986.

13. S. 10337. Cong. Record (128) (daily ed., August 12, 1982). Cited in Joyce Vialet and Sharon Masanz, *The Immigration Reform and Control Act of 1982 Summary and Debate*, Congressional Reference Service Report No. 83-88 EPW, April 29, 1983, p. 66.

14. Governor Richard D. Lamm and Gary Imhoff. *The Immigration Time Bomb: The Fragmenting of America*. New York, E. P. Dutton, 1985, p. 24.

15. Immigration Reform and Control Act of 1985, Report of the Senate Judiciary Committee 99-132, 99th Cong. 1st Sess. Aug. 28, 1985, p. 5.

16. See Senate Report 99-132, supra, note 14.

17. See Lamm and Imhoff, supra, p. 10.

18. 102 S. Ct. 2382 (1982).

19. Statement of Richard Lamm, *Economic and Demographic Consequences of Immigration,* Hearings before the Subcommittee on Economic Resources, Competitiveness, of the Joint Economic Committee, 99th Cong., 2nd Sess., May 1986, p. 369.

20. Simpson-Volstead-Mazzoli, editorial, *Wall Street Journal,* July 12, 1987, p. 12.

21. See generally, Thomas Muller and Thomas Espenshade, *The Fourth Wave,* Washington, D.C., Urban Institute Press, 1985.

22. Joint Hearings before the Senate and House Subcommittees on Immigration, 97th Cong., 1st Sess. 1981, p. 149.

23. While IRCA's employer provisions are striking because of the breadth of their coverage, there are two major exemptions from coverage. The first is independent contractors. Following the Internal Revenue Service classification scheme, a contractor's independence will be determined on a case-by-case basis that will take into account whether the contractor works according to his or her "own means and methods" and is "subject to control only as to results."
   A second potentially important exemption suggested by the regulations is for "contract labor or services." The regulatory language strongly suggests that employees provided by temporary service agencies are the responsibility of the company that pays the employees and not the firm that contracts for their services. 52 Fed. Reg. 16,221 (1987).

24. Here the implementing regulations appear to have broadened the application of the law to include some employment activities that Congress meant to exempt. The rules exempt only employment in "domestic service in a private home that is sporadic, irregular or intermittent." The rules imply that casual hires for nondomestic tasks (e.g., a painter hired to paint an owner's home) or any casual hire by a commercial establishment (a temporary secretary who works for a single day) are not exempt. 8 C.F.R. Sec. 274a. 1(h).

25. On this point, see David A. Martin, Major Issues in Immigration Law. In Thomas A. Alienikoff and David A. Martin, eds. *Immigration Process and Policy.* 1987 Supplement. Wirt Publishing Co., St. Paul, Minn. pp. 111-15.

26. IRCA P.L. 96-603 Sec. 274 (A)(b)(1)(A).

27. 3 C.F.R. Sec. 273a. 2(b)(2)(ii).

28. IRCA Sec. 112.

29. IRCA Sec. 274(A)(d)(2)(ii).

30. IRCA Sec. 274(A)(d)(3).

31. IRCA Sec. 274(A)(g)(3).

32. IRCA Sec. 274(A)(g)(4).

33. IRCA Sec. 274(A)(g)(5)(A).

34. IRCA Sec. 274(A)(a)(2).

35. IRCA Sec. 116.

36. IRCA Sec. 274A(j)-(n).

37. IRCA Sec. 274B.

38. IRCA Sec. 274(B)(a)(3).

39. IRCA Sec. 274(B)(a)(1).

40. IRCA Sec. 274(B)(b).

41. This contrasts with IRCA's sanctions provisions that allow no private right of action.

42. IRCA Sec. 274(B)(a)(3)(B)(4).

43. IRCA Sec. 274(B)(a)(2)(A).

44. Richard W. Day, Keynote Address, in Georges Vernez (ed.), *Immigration and International Relations: Proceedings of A Conference on the International Effects of the 1986 Immigration Reform and Control Act (IRCA)*, Program for Research on Immigration Policy, The RAND Corporation and The Urban Institute, JRI-02 (forthcoming, 1990).

45. Day, 1990.

46. Day, 1990.

47. Day, 1990.

Chapter Three

IMPLEMENTATION CHALLENGES

CHALLENGES TO IRCA'S IMPLEMENTERS

As INS officials set out to implement IRCA, they faced the problem of how to administer a vast new regulatory program under intense political scrutiny. In this chapter we identify the main challenges that faced IRCA's implementers and outline some of the strategies adopted to meet them. The four basic challenges we have identified include:

1. establishing and sustaining the legitimacy of sanctions as a regime for regulating business;

2. satisfying exacting legal requirements that attach to business regulation (and generally apply with less power to the U.S. government's relations with immigrants);

3. adapting the INS as an organization accustomed to dealing with individual immigrants to one capable of educating, regulating, inspecting, and sanctioning businesses;

4. regulating a vast economic process with limited investigative and enforcement resources.

Establishing and Sustaining Legitimacy

IRCA imposed burdens on all employers, requiring that they keep new records and submit to inspections, and depriving some of traditional sources of labor. This broad expansion of regulatory authority was enacted in a pro-business, antiregulatory era, with implementation ultimately overseen by presidents who had been closely identified with the movement to deregulate industry. Moreover, sanctions regulated an action (employment of illegal aliens) that many people considered morally neutral rather than reprehensible.[1] Sanctions enforcement, therefore, lacked a strong constituency. Unlike antidiscrimination or environmental laws, only a few interest groups (the Federation for American Immigration Reform and several labor unions) saw themselves as direct beneficiaries of enforcement. And unlike violations of securities or criminal statutes, there is little political value in aggressive, high visibility enforcement.[2]

While the political rewards for strong enforcement were small, the potential liabilities were great. Clumsy or overzealous enforcement could create a backlash from powerful business groups that might in turn create pressure for the repeal or weakening of sanctions. Thus, the question of legitimacy became paramount for the implementers of employer sanctions. The INS, which had long sought an employer sanctions law to complement its traditional alien apprehension functions, had a strong institutional interest in protecting sanctions from political attack. And the Agency's own institutional reputation depended on its performance in implementing sanctions. The INS's past relationships with business focused on forcible removal of undocumented workers, and were thus often confrontational.[3] Even businesses that had not dealt directly with the INS knew that it had been broadly criticized for unscrupulous enforcement practices in other contexts.

Thus, the INS had to expect to operate under intense and sometimes skeptical scrutiny from Congress, the GAO, the press, the immigration bar, the human rights community, business, and even the private research community.

The challenge of legitimacy required consistent application of clear standards, avoiding complaints of selective enforcement or settling old scores. Legitimacy required that the INS mitigate employer time and cost burdens, take responsibility for employer education, help employers who wanted to stop depending on illegal immigrant employees, and emphasize negotiated compliance rather than penalties.

Finally, sanctions implementation would be judged in part in terms of its effect on other IRCA goals and programs, especially legalization. Enforcement would have to be managed in a way that did not frighten eligible aliens from applying under the legalization program. At minimum, this meant that the profile of the enforcement effort should be kept low and that actions would have to take place well away from the legalization centers.

Satisfying Unfamiliar Legal Requirements

IRCA's implementers faced the challenge of conforming their enforcement of sanctions to the requirements of U.S. constitutional, criminal and administrative laws that would constrain any effort to regulate U.S. firms and citizens. These mandates make more rigorous demands of government actions than those embedded in U.S. immigration laws, which traditionally accord fewer protections to those challenging INS action. Peter Schuck has explained the importance of this distinction:

> Immigration law has long been a maverick, a wild card, in our public law. Probably no other area of

American law has been so radically insulated and divergent from those fundamental norms of constitutional right, administrative procedure, and judicial role that animate the rest of our legal system. In a legal firmament transformed by revolutions in due process and equal protection doctrine and by a new conception of judicial role, immigration law remains the realm in which government authority is at the zenith, and individual entitlement is at the nadir.[4]

The distinctiveness of immigration law lies in the fact that it represents the terms set by the state for entry and citizenship. Therefore, it regulates the rights and entitlements of aliens who, by definition, "lack full membership in the moral and political communities that create and sustain our system of justice."[5] IRCA's employer requirements, by contrast, create obligations for individuals and entities who do hold full membership in the nation's moral and political community and are, thus, entitled to full protections of the system of justice. The INS could expect that the rights extended to employers would likely be fully exercised. At the same time, the Agency had no reason to expect the level of judicial deference that had historically characterized court review of actions against immigrants.[6] These higher legal standards would influence the initiation, conduct, and resolution of enforcement actions.

Three of the most demanding legal challenges faced by sanctions' implementers are announced by IRCA itself. First, the law specifies that hearings contesting charges brought under both IRCA's sanctions and nondiscrimination provisions will be conducted according to the dictates of the Administrative Procedure Act (APA).[7] In practice, this means that administrative hearings resemble trial-type actions brought in the federal courts, governed by federal evidentiary rules and the Federal Rules of Civil Procedure with extensive procedural rights (cross-examination, discovery, notice, record, etc.) accorded defendants. This is in contrast to the informal practices and procedures that govern in most proceedings before immigration judges and in the IRCA legalization program.[8] Compliance with the APA requires that the INS meet the same standards as other federal agencies seeking civil penalties under federal regulatory statutes. It means that the entire enforcement process--targeting, investigations, evidence gathering, and formulation of charges--must anticipate challenges at trial.

Second, IRCA imposes for the first time a requirement that INS agents must have either a warrant or consent before they can conduct an open field or ranch check.[9] Hence Congress, responding to pressures from the agricultural community, extended to agricultural employers protections that exceed those required under the Fourth Amendment of the Constitution.[10]

Third, IRCA authorized penalties against only those employers who could be shown to have knowingly hired an undocumented alien.[11] This requirement imposes a difficult burden of proof on the INS, making enforcement frequently rely on employers' admissions or on the testimony of undocumented workers. In the latter case, the INS must balance its responsibility for removing illegal aliens from the United States against the need to keep them available to provide evidence against their employers. In this way, IRCA creates more difficult problems of proof than most federal agencies typically face.

The enforcement process would also need to conform to generally applicable legal norms, most notably the body of Fourth Amendment case law pertaining to search and seizure and associated warrant requirements that have been so influential in civil and criminal law. Indeed, IRCA might eventually give rise to litigation leading to changes in Fourth Amendment doctrine, as IRCA, for the first time, makes employers both civilly and criminally liable for hiring undocumented workers. Because the law increases their exposure to government enforcement actions, employers are likely to challenge the legality of government searches and subpoenas.[12]

Finally, IRCA's implementers would need to keep the enforcement process itself out of harm's way. Federal agencies implementing IRCA are subject to the Equal Access to Justice Act, under which private parties can recover fees and expenses when a government-initiated legal action is determined not to be "substantially justified."[13] Thus, inept or abusive enforcement practices could lead to claims for damages being filed against the INS and its staff.

Together, these legal and procedural constraints pose a number of challenges. The INS needed to carefully control early litigation to avoid setting precedents that would erode rather than strengthen the regulatory regime. This argued against leaving much discretion to field investigators, at least during the early phases of implementation. Furthermore, given complications introduced by IRCA's exemptions regarding employment of independent contractors and the likely restructuring of businesses to escape liability, INS agents and attorneys would need to master business, agency, and contracts law.

Adapting INS to Serve a New Purpose

Sanctions enforcement would require fundamental changes in the INS's operating style. Agents would have to go beyond the normal daily activity of apprehending undocumented aliens and develop the investigative skills needed to examine complex personnel and financial records. This, in turn, would require that the Agency establish new procedures, recruit and train staff in new techniques, and change its incentive structure to reflect new responsibilities and political expectations.

In addition, the INS would have to adapt an organization designed to foster local initiative and innovation to one that required substantial standardization of policy and procedure. Sanctions policy would have to be made and implemented within the framework of the INS's decentralized structure. The Agency had historically delegated significant discretion, both in policymaking and operations, to its 4 regional, 33 district, and 22 Border Patrol sector offices. This raised the possibility that national implementation strategies, carefully constructed to meet legitimacy and legality imperatives, could be undone by independent local action. Furthermore, sanctions enforcement would require that the Border Patrol and Investigations divisions act in a more coordinated manner, especially in those urban areas where they share a common jurisdiction.

Mounting an Effective Enforcement Process with Limited "Investigative Resources"

Because many undocumented immigrants are employed by small, informally organized firms and because Congress wanted to avoid imposing burdens inequitably, employer sanctions apply to all hiring transactions. As a result, the law's prohibitions and verification requirements extend not only to the nation's seven million firms, but to all individuals entering into employer-employee relationships. Regulation that reaches individual conduct is rare in U.S. administrative and regulatory law.[14] Regulatory schemes with such broad coverage raise questions about the feasibility of law enforcement. As Professor Schuck has written:

> Other things being equal, the more numerous the firms, people or processes that must be regulated, the

> less likely it is that regulation will be effective. . . . If scarce regulatory resources are to be spread over a large number of entities, inspection and monitoring become sporadic, thereby diminishing the credibility of regulatory sanctions. . . . The number of entities may be so great as to make it difficult or impractical for the regulatory agency even to identify, much less regulate them all.[15]

Given the scale of the regulatory enterprise, it was clear that the Agency would have to use its limited enforcement resources efficiently. This would require a strategic use of information as well as manpower in order to obtain voluntary compliance. It would also mean that the Agency should attempt to leverage and coordinate the complementary efforts of enforcement staffs outside the INS that had been enlisted in the sanctions implementation effort, including the Department of Labor's inspection staff and lawyers in U.S. attorneys' offices.

To some extent, the INS's response to the scale of the enforcement mission it confronted would be compromised by the proliferation of enforcement responsibilities taken on by the Agency during the decade. These included enforcement of the 1986 Immigration Marriage Fraud Amendments, the Anti-Drug Abuse Acts of 1986 and 1988, and participation in the Organized Crime and Drug Enforcement Task Force (OCDETF). Competing missions would claim staff hours that could be devoted to sanctions and crowd out the publicity campaigns dedicated to legalization, sanctions, and IRCA's nondiscrimination provisions.

Mitigating the problems posed by scale and resources, the implementers could rely on the fact that a relatively small proportion of U.S. firms depended on undocumented employees, and that some of them would opt to comply voluntarily with the law. As one commentator has written:

Enforcement, happily, is not the sole means of assuring compliance with regulatory directives. Businesses obey regulations for a host of reasons--moral or intellectual commitment to underlying regulatory objectives, belief in the fairness of procedures that produced the regulations, pressure from peers, competitors, customers or employees, conformity with a law-abiding self-image--in addition to fear of detection and punishment.[16]

NATIONAL POLICY RESPONSES TO THE CHALLENGES

The national leaders of the INS are ultimately accountable for the quality and effectiveness of employer sanctions implementation, but they do not deal directly with employers or immigrants. Direct day-to-day contacts are managed by regional and district offices. National leaders in Washington can provide guidance and incentives, but they must rely on their local agents to cope successfully with challenges such as those discussed in the previous section. After describing how administrative responsibility for IRCA is allocated, we discuss a set of national policy decisions taken at the administrative level for sanctions implementation that respond to the challenges described above.

Administrative Responsibility

IRCA assigns responsibility for enforcing civil sanctions to two federal agencies, the INS and the Department of Labor (DOL), with the INS bearing the heaviest enforcement responsibility.

The INS is both a service and a law enforcement agency and its structure reflects these dual missions. Figure 3.1 displays the organization of the INS central office; regional and local district offices are organized in much the same way. The enforcement side of the Agency is responsible for administering sanctions; two of the six units in the Enforcement Division (on the far left of figure 3.1), Investigations and the Border Patrol, assume the lead in educating employers, verifying their compliance and proposing sanctions against violators. The other INS unit with major enforcement responsibility is the General Counsel's Office, which prosecutes violators of civil sanctions and determines whether cases against suspected violators are strong enough to withstand judicial scrutiny.

Historically, the Investigations and Border Patrol divisions have been distinguished by their geographic scope. The Patrol has concentrated on the nation's border regions, ports of entry, and agricultural areas, while the Investigations division has concentrated its efforts in urban areas, working out of offices in most major U.S. cities, both on the border and in the interior. In recent years, however, the Border Patrol has opened new offices in cities such as Dallas, Houston, and San Antonio. This has eliminated the neat geographic distinction between the areas policed by the Border Patrol and those monitored by Investigations.

At the local office level, the principal activities of Investigations and Border Patrol differ. The Border Patrol's traditional assignment has been line watch--a mission that involves the interdiction, capture, and expulsion of illegal immigrants entering without inspection on

Figure 3.1 STRUCTURE OF THE INS

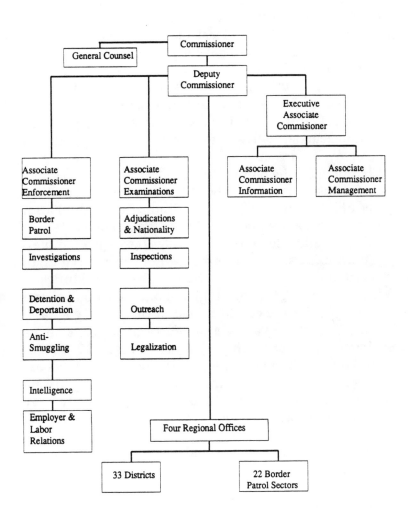

or near the border. By contrast, the Investigations division, as its name suggests, has focused on investigative activities, ferreting out illegal aliens who might be living and working in urban areas. One respondent likened the Border Patrol to "cops on the beat" and Investigations staff to "detectives." Because investigations is viewed as a more complex and sophisticated task than "interdiction," Investigations staff have had to meet higher entry requirements and have typically received higher GS grade levels and pay than Border Patrol staff. In recent years, however, the investigations/interdiction distinction has become blurred, as Border Patrol staff have become increasingly involved in criminal and drug law enforcement and implementation of employer sanctions.

Historically, the Border Patrol's line watch and interdiction functions have been the INS central mission and the basis of its public image. By tradition, the Border Patrol receives the lion's share of the INS enforcement budget.

Organizationally, the INS operates through a complex, decentralized structure composed of central, regional, district, and Border Patrol offices. The central office in Washington and the four regional offices set policy and oversee performance. But most of the Agency's daily business takes place at the local offices, as 90 percent of its staff members work at the 33 district offices and 22 Border Patrol offices. Because these district and sector offices are charged with enforcing the law and providing direct services, and must decide thousands of cases daily, they have exercised an unusually large degree of independent discretion.[17]

Not only are the regions and districts largely autonomous, but within each locality, the three divisions charged with sanctions enforcement--the Border Patrol, Investigations, and the district counsel's office--operate independently of one another to a significant degree. While Border Patrol staff report to the sector chief, Investigations agents report to the district director, and staff attorneys report to the district counsel, who in turn report to the regional counsel (and *not* the district director or the sector chief).

As we indicate above, IRCA also enlists the Department of Labor in the enforcement of sanctions. Two components of DOL's Employment Standards Administration are involved. One is the Wage and Hour (W&H) Division, which enforces a wide range of laws regulating wages and working conditions. The other is the Office of Federal Contract Compliance (OFCCP), which enforces federal regulations that bar federal contractors from discriminating on the basis of race, sex, religion, or national origin.

Under an agreement with the INS, the DOL notifies the INS of apparent violations of IRCA's sanctions and non-discrimination provisions that its inspectors find during the course of routine inspections. The INS is then responsible for all follow-up enforcement activity. It was not assumed that sanctions enforcement would impose substantial new responsibilities on the DOL. Congress appropriated only five million dollars for the DOL in FY 1990 to enable it to increase its enforcement staff by 91 positions to carry out new responsibilities under IRCA.[18]

The enforcement of IRCA's criminal sanctions provisions falls to U.S. attorneys' offices, where INS staff lawyers are assigned to serve as special assistant U.S. attorneys. In addition to their criminal law enforcement charge, these special assistant U.S. attorneys are responsible for handling all other INS matters that involve the federal courts, such as the enforcement of federal administrative subpoenas. Though these lawyers are supervised by the U.S. Attorney, they are paid by the INS and, at least in theory, are pledged to devote a significant share of their time to sanctions and other immigration matters.

As the previous chapter explained, the coordination of these diverse and independent actors would be a major challenge to IRCA's implementers. The autonomous INS Investigations, Border Patrol, and General Counsel's offices, and the DOL Wage and Hour Division, all needed to develop common understandings of the law, what protections to accord employers, what constitutes a violation that warrants follow-up, ways to report compliance and noncompliance and, simply, how to divide the enforcement territory.

The Enforcement Process

The results of the national-level policymaking process can best be understood through a description of what we construe as the officially prescribed model for identifying and penalizing firms that employ illegal aliens.

Figure 3.2 sets out in skeletal form an enforcement action that follows the official policies and guidelines set by the INS central office. This model process, which we have assembled from the INS Field Manual for Employer Sanctions, internal INS memoranda, and interviews in INS central and field offices[19] represents a civil administrative action under IRCA. Criminal actions under IRCA's "pattern and practice" or "harboring and transporting" provisions would use a somewhat different process.

Like all enforcement actions, this process begins with the selection of a party to be investigated. The target can be identified from leads or complaints supplied by sources such as:

- a tip from someone in a position to know whether a firm's employees are undocumented-- often a disgruntled employee;

- an undocumented immigrant who has been apprehended by the INS;

Figure 3.2   THE OFFICIAL ENFORCEMENT PROCESS

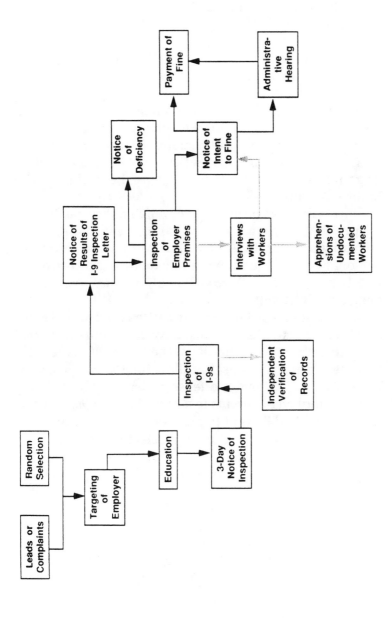

- inspection reports from DOL staff;

- observations made during the course of an INS education visit;

- a petition for a visa submitted by an employer for an undocumented worker.

Alternatively, the employer's name can be drawn at random from a list of all local employers (this approach is known as the General Administrative Plan) or from a list of local employers in industries that have historically hired large numbers of undocumented workers (the Special Emphasis Plan).

Once a firm has been "targeted," INS policy has been to ensure that its owners or managers understand their obligations under IRCA. This is accomplished through a personal visit or telephone call made by a member of the INS Investigations, Border Patrol, or Employer Labor Relations (ELR) staff.

After the education visit or call has been made, the employer is provided a notice informing him or her that following three working days, the INS will inspect the firm's I-9 forms. A refusal to allow the INS to review the I-9s is itself an actionable offense under IRCA. Assuming that the employer consents to a review of its I-9s, when on the premises, INS agents may ask for the employer's payroll records, ask to question selected employees, or request a list of all employees and their dates of hire. The employer can choose to comply with these requests but is entitled to demand that the agent first obtain a warrant or subpoena.

Once the INS has reviewed the I-9s for any possible deficiencies (for instance, incomplete forms, no forms for some employees hired after November 1986, questionable identification documents, or potentially false alien verification numbers), the agent will verify the I-9s or other employment records against data in the INS's computerized Central Index System.

The results of the inspection and computer check are reported to the employer in a Notice of Results of Inspection (NRI) letter. The letter can be sent by mail or delivered by an agent. An employer who is thus informed of a deficiency in his records has 30 to 60 days to respond, either by obtaining further documentation on employees whose status is questionable or by firing unauthorized workers.

If there is reason to suspect a violation, an INS agent conducts a follow-up inspection. The inspection will include another check of the firm's I-9s and might also involve the seizure and review of payroll records, a search of the nonpublic areas of the firm, the questioning of employees (again with consent of the employer or by means of a warrant), and the possible apprehension of undocumented workers. Apprehended workers are interviewed and their statements transcribed. In some instances, they will be removed from the country. In others, at the INS's discretion, they can be released but given "voluntary departure," that is, a requirement to leave the U.S. on their own by a designated date.

At this point, INS inspectors may determine that the employer has reformed his hiring practices and that no further violations are likely. The INS can close the case by issuing a "notice of deficiency" letter, identifying the employer's violations and recording his assurance of future compliance. This letter has no legal force, but it could become a factor in future proceedings against an employer who is found to revert to the practice of hiring illegal aliens.

Following analysis of the statements and evidence, the INS can then issue a Notice of Intent to Fine (NIF), setting out the character of violations charged and assessing a fine for each violation. If the violation occurred between June 1, 1987 and May 31, 1988, and if the employer had not been previously charged with a violation of IRCA, the INS can issue a citation or warning rather than assess a fine. An employer who has previously received a citation will be fined. IRCA makes no provision for appeals of citations.

If the employer does not challenge the NIF within 45 days, a Final Order is entered. The Final Order cannot be appealed. If the employer challenges the NIF, the INS can file a complaint with the Chief Administrative Hearing Officer of the Department of Justice's Executive Office of Immigration Review, who would, in turn, serve the employer with the complaint. After a response from the employer, the case proceeds to a hearing. Most challenged NIFs, however, are expected to be settled through negotiation prior to an administrative hearing.

Hearings are held before an administrative law judge and are conducted in accordance with the dictates of the Administrative Procedures Act (APA). Following a hearing, a written decision is rendered on the charges. The decision of the administrative law judge is then reviewed by the Chief Administrative Hearing Officer, who can modify, vacate, or sustain it. Either party can appeal that decision to the U.S. Court of Appeals. If the INS's complaint is upheld and no appeal is requested, a Final Order is then issued.

Key Policy Decisions

In the following pages we analyze some key aspects of the enforcement process in greater detail. We focus on the ways in which INS officials made conscious efforts to respond to the four challenges of legitimacy, legality, institutional change, and scope. We do not comment on those elements of the enforcement process where the INS central office has, for all practical purposes, been silent or where "policies" represent a simple restatement of IRCA or of established case law.

A concern for establishing the legitimacy of employer sanctions is the most fundamental challenge, and it has clearly driven the design of the enforcement process. Efforts to respond to other challenges are subordinated to (and frequently embedded within) the efforts to ensure that sanctions enforcement will be seen as balanced, fair, and moderate. The enforcement process mandated by INS's national office:

- reflects a solicitude for the subjects of regulation, ensuring that employers receive notice of their responsibilities and advice about methods of compliance, and are protected against selective targeting and vindictive enforcement;

- gives employers multiple opportunities to comply with the law and avoid punishment;

- emphasizes the detection and punishment of substantive, knowing violations, not technical "paperwork" violations;

- places ultimate control over the imposition of penalties in the hands of attorneys rather than inspectors.

Educating the Employer. Few recent regulatory laws emphasize information and education as IRCA does. As we have indicated, Congress did not expect INS to engage in confrontational or punitive enforcement. The implementers consequently had to rely on cheaper and less bruising ways of encouraging compliance, and education was the obvious approach.

It was, moreover, reasonable to expect that employers would need education, since IRCA outlawed a practice--hiring undocumented aliens--that had been broadly adopted and legally permitted. A special Employer Labor Relations (ELR) branch was created within the INS, and a major share of INS field inspectors' time in 1987 and 1988 was dedicated to visiting employers, providing explanatory materials, and answering questions. The concern for legitimacy also drove the INS's efforts to advise employers who needed to find new labor supplies and, in some cases, to find sources of legal low-wage workers (e.g., among legal refugee groups or mildly retarded adults).

Shortly after IRCA was enacted, former INS Commissioner Alan Nelson directed that no investigation could be undertaken or citation issued until the employer had received an educational visit from an INS officer.[20] The education visit was thus transformed from a discretionary act of administrative courtesy to a pre-condition of enforcement.[21] Nelson's mandate established a new first step, at least for enforcement actions conducted soon after the law's enactment. (It remains to be seen whether the education requirement continues after employers have had several years to become familiar with the law).

The education visit serves other purposes in addition to safeguarding legitimacy. It strengthens the enforcement process. An INS agent's educational visit to an employer establishes the employer's knowledge of the law. This greatly strengthens the INS's hand in any dispute over whether the employer knowingly hired an undocumented worker. Educational visits also provide leads for investigations. Observations made during the course of an educational visit--foreign names on a firm's time cards, for example--can trigger follow-up investigations.[22]

The education visit, then, is both a method for obtaining voluntary compliance and a way of targeting future investigations and building cases against potential violators. Its use in these diverse ways reflects the tension between enforcing IRCA and mitigating its impact.

Targeting Enforcement Actions. INS strategy for targeting employer investigations has to serve several purposes. It has to avoid charges of selective enforcement against any class of employers, yet demonstrate the INS's diligence in enforcement; it has to be legally defensible; and it has to make efficient use of limited investigative resources.

With these considerations in mind, the INS created a targeting strategy that emphasizes: (1) random inspections conducted according to the General Administrative Plan or Special Emphasis Plan, and (2) lead-driven investigations.

The random targeting plan was introduced by the INS in February 1988. It is directly modeled on the Occupational Safety and Health Administration's two-track system for random targeting of employers. One set of employers is drawn randomly from a list of all U.S. firms (this list is called the General Administrative Plan, or GAP). A second set of employers is drawn at random from lists of firms in local industries that have traditionally employed large numbers of undocumented aliens. (The latter is called the Special Emphasis Plan, or SEP list). SEP targeting is tailored to each locality; the factors used to identify target industries are designated by the local INS district or Border Patrol office. To avoid local bias in targeting, the SEP lists are drawn by the INS central office in Washington.

Random targeting was intended to achieve several objectives. On the one hand, it was expected to send a strong signal that targeting would be based on neutral principles and not driven by an interest in settling old scores. Second, random targeting offered a means for the Agency to monitor evolving patterns of compliance and non-compliance across industries and regions, making the enforcement process more efficient. Third, public knowledge of a randomized targeting process could increase the effectiveness of the entire enforcement process, as awareness of the mere existence of such a program may induce voluntary compliance among risk-averse firms. In practice, because few employers targeted by the GAP have ever employed undocumented aliens, inspections can be completed quickly; the INS is therefore able to demonstrate its diligence by reporting large numbers of inspections completed.

Establishment of the random targeting policy intensified the challenge of adapting the INS organization to serve new purposes. While regional and national officials had strong incentives to guarantee the rationality, restraint, and fairness of the enforcement program, field agents were accustomed to working under very different incentives. Based on Agency tradition, they expected to be judged by the numbers of violations discovered and penalties imposed. For such agents, random targeting was a waste of time because compared to lead-generated investigations, it was unlikely to generate large numbers of penalties.

While random GAP inspections limit agents' discretion in targeting, lead-driven inspections expand it. The standard of proof required to justify an investigation--the "ability to articulate logical reasons to suspect a violation"[23]--is not demanding, and the number of leads available at any time vastly exceeds available manpower capacities. Furthermore, while random inspections detect relatively few violations and produce few penalties, lead-driven investigations tend to increase those outcomes. Colin Diver has written:

> The tendency of inspectors' superiors to judge their performance by quantitative, rather than qualitative, indicators reinforces their reliance on private tips. Whatever may be said for its impact on enforcement quality, a complaint-based policy is often a reliable

tactic for maximizing the quantity of violations discovered. Unless a sizable number of complainants file complaints solely to harass regulated firms, it is safe to assume that the probability of finding a violation in response to a complaint is higher than in a random inspection.[24]

INS national policy has sought to balance the pressures for random and lead-driven targeting. Forty percent of the time spent on employer sanctions investigations is to be dedicated to firms targeted by the GAP. Of that 40 percent, half is to be applied to firms drawn randomly and half to firms in targeted industries. National INS policy permits staff to devote the remaining 60 percent of time to investigations following leads.

Developing and Bringing a Case. Once a probable violation is discovered, the INS must still try to safeguard its implementation processes against charges of abuse. It has tried to forestall complaints by giving employers advance notice of records inspections. To avoid charges of employer harassment, national directives have urged that enforcement focus on knowing substantive violations, not on paperwork technicalities. To ensure the legal propriety of its investigations and penalty processes, the INS has put investigators under the ultimate supervision of Agency attorneys.

The importance of mitigating the burden of enforcement on employers led the INS to require that employers receive three days' notice of an inspection of their I-9s.[25] This requirement is more lenient than the enforcement practices of most regulatory agencies, including the most similar regulatory program, the Department of Labor's enforcement of the Wage and Hour laws.[26]

Like the policy requiring education visits before investigations, the three-day notice requirement mitigates the potentially confrontational character of the enforcement process. The three-day notice can be eliminated, however, when INS agents are able to obtain a civil or criminal search warrant based on probable cause to believe that a violation of the employer requirements is taking place.

Viewed from another perspective, this lenient policy on notice can be seen as compensating for IRCA's stern requirement that the employers provide INS agents access to their I-9s without a search warrant. Moreover, the law makes failure to provide access a separate, actionable offense that carries a civil fine.[27]

The need to deal with U.S. citizens and firms likely to exercise their rights represented a major challenge to the INS. One policy response advocated by the General Counsel's Office was to require that all NIFs be signed by a member of the district counsel's staff before they could be issued. The NIF is the charging document in a sanctions case, and control over whether it is issued and its content represents a real transfer of power within the INS from local inspectors to Agency lawyers.[28] To illustrate, the NIF differs from an Order to Show Cause Not to be Deported, which is the charging document in a typical alien-focused legal action. The latter is generally signed by the district director designee rather than the district counsel.

IRCA's employer requirements establish a hierarchy of penalties. Paperwork violations carry the lowest fines. Paperwork violations are easy to prove; in contrast, it is difficult to prove that an employer has knowingly hired an illegal alien. Pursuing paperwork violations can be a useful strategy for obtaining voluntary compliance and for seasoning an inexperienced enforcement staff. However, INS emphasis on paperwork violations could be taken as employer harassment or as a sign of a trivial enforcement effort.

The INS has taken what appears on the face of it to be a strong policy on paperwork-only violations, stating that the focus of sanctions enforcement was to be on knowing, substantive violations and that the use of paperwork-only violations should be limited to cases where the violation is either "egregious" or where the fine is "appended to" or in lieu of a knowing violation.[29] To date, however, no definition has been developed for an "egregious" violation by national policy staff, despite (as the next chapter will document) wide variation in regional practices and broad use of paperwork-only violations.

INS FUNDING

The character of employer sanctions implementation was profoundly affected by resource allocation decisions made in Congress and within the INS. These decisions gave concrete meaning to Congress's intention to constrain the INS from hyperactive enforcement of employer sanctions. But these decisions went further, to signal that sanctions must take a back seat to the funding of more traditional INS functions.

IRCA authorized substantial new resources for the INS: $422 million in fiscal year 1987 and $419 in fiscal year 1988, representing roughly a 70 percent increase in the overall Agency budget. Employer sanctions was only one of several INS activities with a claim on these resources. As it turned out, a combination of congressional initiatives and internal INS priority setting gave enforcement of sanctions only one quarter of the new funds to be dedicated to enforcement.

A provision known as the Moorhead Amendment, added during debate on the floor of the House of Representatives, directed that the INS spend as much of the additional funds authorized by IRCA as necessary to increase Border Patrol staffing in 1987 and 1988 by 50 percent over its 1986 level. Though the amendment was not binding on the INS, it kept the politically popular Border Patrol at the front of the INS funding queue. Another provision of the law, which received comparatively little legislative attention but would absorb enforcement resources, was the MacKay Amendment (Section 701), which stated that the INS should expeditiously remove criminal aliens from the United States.

Once IRCA was enacted, one of the INS's first implementation tasks was to request supplemental appropriations for the funds authorized by IRCA. The 1987 supplemental request was for $147 million, of which $132 million was for enforcement. Only 26 percent of the extra $132 million sought for enforcement would go to sanctions. Border control, which already claimed 42 percent of the 1987 INS enforcement budget, would absorb 53 percent of the extra enforcement money. Another share (13 percent) of the new enforcement money would be used to implement the MacKay Amendment.

The Moorhead and MacKay amendments directed the lion's share of new funds to the Border Patrol, which was intended to play a relatively minor part in employer sanctions implementation, and away from the Investigations division, which bore primary responsibility for sanctions. Before IRCA, the Border Patrol was by far the largest division of the INS. To illustrate, in 1986 the Border Patrol received $164 million and 3,639 work years, while Investigations received $44 million and 789 work years. Investigations had been steadily trimmed in the prior decade, falling from 1,377 agents in 1978 to 789 in 1987. If legislators were to fulfill the Moorhead Amendment's goal of a 50 percent increase in the Border Patrol, it was a foregone conclusion that the Patrol would absorb the largest share of IRCA resources because its initial funding base was the biggest.

While the Border Patrol received the largest share of enforcement resources following IRCA, Investigations' manpower and resources also grew rapidly, albeit from a low base. By 1990 the Agency was requesting 1,738 positions for Investigations, 932 of which had been added following IRCA, representing a doubling of the division's size. At the same time, the Agency was requesting 4,941 positions within the Border Patrol. While the disparity between the manpower of Investigations and the Border Patrol remained large, it had narrowed somewhat in relative terms since 1986.

The INS's decision to devote a significant share of IRCA resources to the removal of criminal aliens also reflects how the Agency's previous priorities shaped the implementation of IRCA. Removal of criminal aliens had received high priority beginning in 1983, when the Investigations division implemented a policy of focusing resources on the most significant cases.[30] As the 1980s progressed, the criminal alien issue became even more important as concern grew about drug trafficking and prison overcrowding. Even though the INS's request for $17 million for removal of criminal aliens represented only a small share of the IRCA enforcement package, the policy was important because the Investigations division bore primary responsibility for it. Indeed, 345 of the 932 new Investigations positions requested following IRCA would be dedicated to criminal aliens, while only 500 would be devoted to sanctions. Thus, sanctions would be competing with another major new program for investigative time.

In the next chapter, we examine ways in which these policies and congressional concerns have been interpreted at the local level. The analysis will also highlight important variations in local policy such as:

- whether the employer sanctions enforcement process is seen principally as an opportunity to apprehend illegal aliens or as a way to influence employers' hiring practices;

- the degree to which analysis of employer records (e.g., I-9 forms), or the testimony of apprehended aliens is used as the engine of the enforcement process;

- different degrees of emphasis on criminal sanctions under IRCA's pattern and practice and harboring and transporting provisions.

Notes, chapter three

1. Three years after IRCA's enactment, some local governments are still helping undocumented aliens find jobs. See, for example, Los Angeles Project Aids Illegal Aliens, in Challenge to U.S., *New York Times*, October 26, 1989, p. 1.

2. This was not the case with regard to the enforcement of IRCA's antidiscrimination provisions, where powerful interest groups like the Mexican American Legal Defense and Education Fund (MALDEF) and La Raza did view their constituents as being protected by vigorous enforcement.

3. See, for example, J. Crewdson, *The Tarnished Door: The New Immigrants and the Transformation of America*. New York, Times Books, 1983, pp. 113-141.

4. Peter Schuck, The Transformation of Immigration Law, 84 Col. L. Rev. 1, (1984).

5. Ibid.

6. While Schuck notes that judicial deference to congressional and administrative action in immigration policy has begun to

break down, for almost a century the courts' deference to the political branch and to administrative expertise was striking, especially when viewed alongside other areas of public law where that deference was often more rhetorical than real. Supra, pp. 14-17.

7. Title 8 USC Sec. 1324a(e)(3)(B) requires that in an employer sanctions case, "the hearing shall be conducted in accordance with the requirements of 5 USC 554."

8. These procedures have been broadly challenged. See, for example, *Haitian Refugee Center, Inc. v. Nelson*, 872 F. 2d 1555 (11th Cir. 1989) holding, among other things, that legalization offices had to make available translators in Spanish and Haitian Creole, that applicants had to be afforded the opportunity to present witnesses at their interviews, and that the interviewers had to "particularize the evidence offered, testimony taken, credibility determinations, and any other relevant information" on the worksheets prepared following the interview that recommended approval or denial of the legalization application. 66 Interpreter Releases, 745, July 10, 1989.

9. INA Sec. 287(e); (a)(3) Provides that an immigration officer may not enter the premises of a farm or other outdoor agricultural operation for the purpose of interrogating a person believed to be an alien regarding his right to be in the United States absent the consent of the owner or a properly executed warrant.

10. In *Oliver vs. United States* 466 S. Ct. 170 (1984) the Supreme Court affirmed that warrantless searches onto open fields did not violate the Fourth Amendment's ban on unreasonable searches and seizures.

11. This knowledge requirement also serves to distinguish IRCA from most other regulatory regimes, which do not require knowledge to make out a substantive violation of the statute. Two exceptions are the Walsh-Healy Act of June 30, 1936 (41 USCA Secs. 35-45) barring the knowing employment of male children under age 16 by an agency or instrumentality of the U.S. in the manufacture of supplies and equipment exceeding $10,000. The

1972 Consumer Product Safety Act (15 USC Sec. 2051 et. seq.) bars the manufacture, distribution, or sale of hazardous products and makes parties "knowingly" in violation of the Act subject to civil penalties.

12. See, for example, In Re: Subpoena of Gilbert Ramirez, Misc. No. Ty.-89-00023 (E.D. Tex., March 15, 1989), holding that only administrative law judges have the power to issue subpoenas under IRCA Section 101, and granting the employer's motion to quash an INS subpoena.

13. 5 USC 504 (1985).

14. For example, the Occupational Safety and Health Act of 1970, P.L. 91-596, restricts coverage to firm-level behavior.

15. Peter Schuck, Regulation: Asking the Right Questions, *The National Journal,* April 28, 1979, p. 712.

16. Colin S. Diver, A Theory of Regulatory Enforcement, 28 Public Policy, 297, 1980.

17. This material has been drawn from Jason Juffras, *The 1986 Immigration Reform and Control Act and Its Impact on the Immigration and Naturalization Service,* Program for Research on Immigration Policy, The RAND Corporation and The Urban Institute, Spring 1990.

18. From September 1, 1987 through August 31, 1988, the W&H conducted I-9 inspections at 28,420 places of employment; the OFCCP conducted inspections at 2,364 such places. The General Accounting Office, Immigration Reform: Status of Implementing Employer Sanctions After Second Year, GGD-89-16, U.S. Government Printing Office, November 1988.

19. INS Immigration Officer's Field Manual for Enforcement of Employer Sanctions, INS Pub. No. M-278, November 30, 1987 (hereafter referred to as Field Manual).

20. "Employer Sanctions Strategy--Employer Visits," Memorandum from INS Commissioner Alan Nelson to INS Regional Commissioners (June 8, 1987), reported on and reproduced at 64 Interpreter Releases 875-76, 889-90 (July 27, 1987).

21. The *Field Manual* states: "Investigations. For investigations, the educational contact must occur prior to the performance of an investigative inspection: a single visit may not be used for both purposes." (Section III-4) Nov. 20, 1987.

22. 3.Id. at III-2, states that one source of leads for targeting investigations should be "derogatory information obtained in the course of employer educational contacts." The example is drawn from field interviews with INS agents.

23. *Field Manual*, INS Pub. No., M-278, November 30, 1978, III-A.

24. Colin S. Diver, A Theory of Regulatory Enforcement, 28 Public Policy, 1980, p. 282.

25. 8 CFR 274a.2(b)(2)(ii).

26. In fact, DOL officials argued against this requirement and, by implication, its application to I-9 inspections conducted by DOL agents. One result of this debate between the INS and DOL is a policy that prohibits INS officers from asking employers to waive the three-day notice for inspection but which expressly permits DOL agents to request a waiver of the notice requirement of employers. See Field Manual, Sections III-C-2 and III-C-3.

27. Some legal scholars have questioned the constitutionality of this provision of the law, arguing that it violates employers' Fourth Amendment rights and that it is inconsistent with recent Supreme Court decisions. Charles Foster, Constitutional and Procedural Issues in INS Enforcement of the Employer Verification and Sanctions Provisions of the Immigration Reform and Control Act of 1986, *Georgetown Immigration Law Journal* 461, Fall 1988.

28. The role of the district or sector counsel was established by interim policy guidance and as of this writing has yet to be overturned. That interim guidance states:

> All Notices of Intent to Fine must, with concurrence of the District or Sector Counsel, be submitted with concurrent copies to the regional office and to Central Office Enforcement for approval, with concurrence of General Counsel. When the District or Sector Counsel does not concur, the officer should submit the application to Central Office Enforcement for information purposes. *Field Manual*, p. III-E-4-b.

29. "The Service's focus is on significant cases involving violations of the prohibitions against knowingly employing unauthorized aliens: Citations and Notices of Intent to Fine may be issued for violations of the verification, or paperwork requirements. Generally, citations and Notices of Intent to Fine for paperwork violations should be appended to substantive violations. However, citations and Notices of Intent to Fine solely for violations of the paperwork requirements may be issued in the following circumstances:

(a) The paperwork violations are egregious, such as willful failure to complete I-9 Forms for new hires following a documented Service educational contact; or

(b) The paperwork violations relate to substantive violations. Substantive charges should include citations and fines for knowingly hiring unauthorized workers. If this cannot be proved, but the apprehension of unauthorized workers at the workplace is involved, paperwork violations can be issued at the discretion of the District Director or Chief Patrol Agent." *Field Manual*, p. III-12.

30. An INS memorandum detailing the Agency's investigative priorities for fiscal year 1983 included the goal of giving "priority to assigning enforcement resources to high-volume/impact workload areas for maximum effectiveness" and the creation of an Investigations Case Management System to guide this effort. The INS's budget request for fiscal year 1985, prepared in

January 1984, noted that Investigations' highest priority level under the case management system "includes those cases targeting criminal aliens."

Chapter Four

IMPLEMENTING SANCTIONS:
REPORTS FROM THE FIELD

IRCA is a safety valve for the U.S. To the guys guarding the border, it gave sanctions and deterrence. To the nuns, it gave legalization.

INS Regional Official

We wanted employer sanctions because we knew we were shovelling sand against the tide just using border apprehensions and deportations as a deterrent.

INS Border Patrol Officer

We're not picking up aliens, we're not doing area control, and we don't send anybody back because there isn't any money.

INS Investigations Agent

You can legislate all you want, but it won't stop the flow of hungry people.

INS Regional Administrator

INTRODUCTION

This chapter reviews the local and regional implementation of IRCA's employer requirements in light of the challenges identified in chapter 3: establishing and sustaining the legitimacy of a new regulatory regime, satisfying exacting legal requirements that are unfamiliar to the implementing agencies, adapting an organization geared to the apprehension of illegal immigrants to the very different task of regulating business, and mounting an effective enforcement effort with limited funds and staff resources.

The findings we report are based on our extensive interviewing in eight cities and in INS regional offices. We also examined written material and regional plans whenever possible. Because we conducted interviews under promise of confidentiality, no respondents are identified by name or other unique descriptors. We use quotes from the interviews whenever they illustrate a key point or encapsulate an important idea. We try to provide a comprehensive picture of the implementation process and to highlight important patterns and unresolved issues.

Three important generalizations emerge from our data.

First, in the communities we visited, the numbers of investigations conducted are low relative to the numbers of employers. While INS Investigations units have been enlarged, INS Investigations staffs, which bear primary enforcement authority, have only returned to the number of agents in place in the mid-1970s after a decade of declining in size. Furthermore, the inexperience of new staff members and competing responsibilities (e.g., for anti-drug and organized crime initiatives and for criminal aliens) have claimed many available resources, thus limiting the effort devoted to sanctions enforcement.

Second, the INS has been circumspect in dealing with most employers and has avoided generating broad public opposition to sanctions enforcement. Individual employers have been investigated and penalized, but actions have not been so widespread or arbitrary as to cause the business community to oppose the sanctions program.

Third, the enforcement effort--and the burden of coping with inspections and fines--falls heavily on small firms owned by ethnics. These firms are also the most likely to be dependent on immigrant labor.

Fourth, we observed significant variation in implementation from site to site. Local INS offices differed with respect to the priority attached to sanctions enforcement, procedures followed, characteristics of firms targeted for enforcement, and the numbers and types of fines imposed. Regarding priorities, some INS local offices saw sanctions as their top enforcement priority, while others focused instead on the pursuit of criminal aliens or drug-related crimes. In terms of practices and procedures, some INS offices dealt with employers through a standard regulatory investigative process, starting with an analysis of business records; other offices made employer sanctions an extension of the traditional INS alien apprehension process, raiding business premises to remove undocumented aliens and investigating firms identified by apprehended aliens as their employers. Some INS offices made employers the primary targets of sanctions enforcement; others used sanctions enforcement as a way to identify undocumented workers for deportation.

Localities also varied in their relative emphasis on fines for paperwork and substantive violations. Criminal sanctions were seldom sought, in part because U.S. attorneys offices are busy prosecuting more sensational and dangerous crimes.

Fifth, poor coordination between INS Investigations and Border Patrol officers has led to different treatment of similar firms within the same geographic area.
The body of this chapter analyzes how sanctions have been implemented in a number of U.S. communities with high concentrations of foreign-born residents. We begin with a brief discussion of the communities we visited, their economic and political contexts, and the resources and staffing local INS offices are able to devote to sanctions enforcement. We then analyze the local enforcement process in terms of goals and priorities, targeting of employers for investigations, and penalties proposed and levied.

THE COMMUNITIES

The eight communities we visited--Los Angeles, San Jose, Houston, San Antonio, El Paso, Miami, New York City, and Chicago--differed dramatically in size, economic and demographic composition, and political climate. The INS establishments in those communities were also highly varied due to differences in proximity to the border and to the local importance of drug and alien smuggling activities.

Size

Communities covered by the INS varied in population size and geographic scope. These factors create very different problems for enforcement. The communities with the largest populations also contain vast numbers of business establishments, presenting a daunting challenge to any inspections program. The INS New York District contains over 500,000 business establishments, and Los Angeles contains more than 325,000. The El Paso District, in contrast, covers fewer than 20,000 business establishments.[1]

Some of the districts with relatively few establishments, however, cover very large territories. The San Antonio District Office sprawls over much of central and southern Texas, reaching from Austin to Corpus Christi and covering 78 counties and 3,000 square miles.

Political Climate

Each of the three largest cities in our sample (Chicago, Los Angeles, and New York) has adopted official or unofficial policies of noncooperation with the INS in the reporting of city residents who are undocumented.[2] Each tacitly or expressly encourages the provision of city services to undocumented residents where not otherwise prohibited by law, and each has been an important actor in litigation to include undocumented immigrants in the 1990 Census.[3] In contrast, many other city governments in our study resemble Houston's, which has been less active in pro-immigrant causes.

The institutionalization of immigrant-serving organizations was an important factor in determining the local political climate. Mature, legally sophisticated organizations scrutinized IRCA implementation closely in Chicago, New York, and Los Angeles.[4] Houston and San Antonio, in contrast, had fewer and less powerful immigrant advocacy organizations.

Traditional INS Missions

INS offices in the different sites had different histories and strong prior commitments to specific tasks. In New York, for example, the defining INS mission has been to ensure that persons arriving from abroad at the city's airports are processed quickly and efficiently. In Miami, the continuing fight against drugs from South and Central America has dominated the INS's attention for several years. In San Jose, due to the proximity of San Quentin prison, the traditional emphasis was on deportation of criminal aliens.

Proximity to the Border

Immigrant apprehension is inevitably a major enterprise in border cities and it affects the character of all INS activities there. The constitutional protections accorded individuals to be free from unreasonable searches and seizures without "probable cause" have less power at the border.[5] Hence, law enforcement tends to be less deferential to constitutional and procedural norms at the border than elsewhere. Furthermore, because of the relatively low cost of removing apprehended aliens from border cities to their source countries, the focus of INS activity tends to be on arrest and deportation of illegal aliens. In interior cities such as Chicago, stronger constitutional protections apply, the costs of deportation are significantly higher, and alien removal is not the dominant priority.

Proximity to the border also influences the degree to which foreign-born populations are settled and have become part of the fabric of the local community. There are obvious differences between recent border-crossers in El Paso and a Polish family that has found its way to an Eastern European enclave in Chicago.

ENFORCEMENT RESOURCES

Initially, following IRCA's enactment, new resources flowed to INS local offices, staff size grew rapidly, and internal growth was supplemented by the involvement of other federal agencies (U.S. attorneys and DOL inspectors) in the enforcement process. However, the impact of increased INS resources and staffing on sanctions enforcement was limited or complicated by emerging budget issues, by the number of competing missions assigned to INS enforcement staff, and by the problem of mobilizing several major initiatives simultaneously.

Local INS Staffing

Sanctions implementation at the local level falls to four branches: Investigations, the Border Patrol, the district and sector counsels' offices, and the newly formed Employer and Labor Relations (ELR) branch. Each of those branches grew significantly at the local level following IRCA's enactment in 1986. In Chicago, for example, the size of the Investigations staff increased from 47 to 86 between 1986 and 1989. In Los Angeles, growth was even more rapid; the size of the Los Angeles District's Investigations staff rose from 35 in 1985 to 152 in 1989, an increase of more than 400 percent.

As table 4.1 shows, staff allocations result in uneven coverage of different jurisdictions. The Los Angeles District Office assigns two staff members to sanctions enforcement per 10,000 local employers; the El Paso District Office assigns eight per 10,000 employers, and the El Paso Border Patrol deploys an additional ten agents per 10,000 employers. In San Jose, our one site where the INS office is only a branch of a distant district office, sanctions

Table 4.1   STAFFING INS EMPLOYER SANCTIONS[a]

Site	Enforcement staff	Sanctions staff	% Sanctions staff	Sanctions staff per 10,000 employers[b]
Los Angeles	152	70	46	2.2
Chicago	86	35	41	2.0
Miami	48	18	38	2.0
San Antonio	36	13	36	4.6
Houston	48	18	31	2.3
New York	156	43	27	0.9
El Paso	39	8	21	8.0
El Paso BP	800	10[c]	4	30.0

a. Data reporting the number of enforcement staff for individual districts is drawn from an unpublished INS document, *Investigations Program: Full-time Permanent Authorized Positions & Staffing Report, as of March 31, 1989. Data on the number of employer sanctions staff on duty were drawn from the second wave of field interviews by study staff conducted during June 1989.*

b. Source: U.S. Bureau of the Census, *County Business Patterns, 1986,* Selected States, U.S. Government Printing Office, Washington, D.C., 1988. See Table 2: Counties--Employees, Payroll and Establishments by Industry: 1986.

c. This figure reflects the number of El Paso Border Patrol staff assigned the same approximate jurisdiction as the El Paso District Office investigating staff.

is staffed at a rate of less than one person per 10,000 employers. In general, communities not served by district offices have far fewer investigators than do the district office cities.

IRCA also had a substantial impact on the size of the Border Patrol.[6] The El Paso Border Patrol sector, for example, added 200 agent positions to bring its authorized force to 800. The Border Patrol assigns a smaller proportion of its staff to sanctions enforcement than does

Investigations. (In the Western Region, for example, only eight percent of Border Patrol staff time is allocated to sanctions.) However, the total force is so large that the number of Border Patrol agents assigned to sanctions may be higher in a particular district than the number of Investigations agents. For example, ten Border Patrol agents have sanctions responsibilities within the El Paso District, as compared to eight district Investigations agents.

INS district counsels' offices also grew rapidly as they were transformed from offices with skeletal staffs to full legal departments. In San Antonio, for example, the district counsel's office grew from four to eleven attorneys. The number of attorneys in El Paso doubled from four to eight; in Houston, the counsel's staff grew from one attorney in 1983 to ten in 1989.

Finally, virtually all district and sector offices have assigned one to two persons to carry out employer education and to serve as ELR officers.

Competing New Missions

To some extent, the staffing of sanctions at the district level reflects choices being made among the number of competing missions that have been assigned to the INS's enforcement personnel in recent years. These include a movement into criminal law enforcement and the removal of criminal aliens from the U.S.,[7] participation in the Organized Crime and Drug Enforcement Task Force (OCDETF),[8] new responsibilities under the Immigration Marriage Fraud Amendments of 1986, and anti-fraud activities, some of which are IRCA-related.[9] As we indicated above, this proliferation of responsibilities assigned to INS enforcement staff subordinated sanctions to one among several competing missions.

At the district level the competition usually had direct implications for the size of the sanctions enforcement staff. Two factors appeared to drive the proportion of enforcement staff dedicated to sanctions: the priority assigned to criminal law enforcement and fraud, and the number of businesses to be regulated. We found that Los Angeles and Chicago devoted the highest shares of total resources to sanctions. In other districts, like El Paso, where efforts to combat drug flows are paramount and where the number of businesses is fewer, the share of resources is lower.

In addition to reducing the manpower available for sanctions enforcement, this competition for resources has led to leadership losses and a brain-drain as the most experienced investigators gravitate to higher prestige activities such as drug law enforcement. In particular, the INS's participation in the OCDETF has attracted many of the Agency's most accomplished agents.

Mobilization

The rapid scale-up in Investigations and Border Patrol personnel in the wake of IRCA's enactment has inevitably raised problems. Though newly hired agents are much more likely than older Agency staff to hold college degrees, they are inexperienced. Virtually all the members of one unit of the Los Angeles employer sanctions staff are new recruits. Managers are reluctant to assign them difficult investigations or sensitive criminal harboring and transporting cases. As an official in another locality noted, "they [the new recruits] cannot understand, much less enforce, the law."

This inexperience may be aggravated by other factors. For example, high turnover in Border Patrol employer sanctions units in the Western Region is slowing the enforcement effort.[10] Furthermore, the large number of new recruits, coupled with the INS budget crisis, have made it difficult to find space for new agents at the government's training academy in Glynco, Georgia.

Budget Crisis

By 1989, the INS was in the midst of a budget crisis precipitated by two events. The first was the surge of Central American immigrants into South Texas, leading to expensive INS efforts to detain the migrants in Texas's Rio Grande Valley, adjudicate their asylum claims and provide transportation home for those deported or accepting "voluntary" departures.[11] The second development was an INS central office decision to implement the Moorhead Amendment and fully fund all authorized staff positions within the Border Patrol, leading to INS-wide cost overruns of several million dollars. This shortfall was partially attributable to the fact that the Agency was expecting to get more money from the 1988 Anti-Drug Abuse Act than it eventually received.

The budget crisis, which hit with full force in the fourth quarter of FY 1989, had different impacts across the eight sites. In Houston it contributed to a decision to sharply curtail sanctions enforcement in favor of less expensive investigative activities, specifically SAW fraud enforcement, which involves less travel and commensurately lower costs. In other localities in the Southern and Western regions, the crisis meant reducing funds for travel and litigation. The El Paso Border Patrol, for example, was considering dropping its largest sanctions case for cost-related reasons. In contrast, the Eastern and Northern regions maintained sanctions as their top priority even while adapting to the Agency-wide hiring freeze.

By June 1989, then, sanctions implementation at the local level was hampered by more than the vicissitudes of growth and proliferating responsibilities. For the first time, the harsh fiscal realities of the Gramm-Rudman era were felt.

THE ENFORCEMENT PROCESS

Local Priorities

INS officials in all sites welcomed employer sanctions as an important new weapon for immigration control. Many INS respondents in our fall 1988 interviews said employer sanctions was their number one priority. However, by the time of our summer 1989 interviews, many of our respondents indicated that employer sanctions had declined as a local enforcement priority. This development was partly due to the fact that the Agency was trying to balance competing enforcement responsibilities.

Characterizing a complex agency's priorities is difficult, because every official has his or her own version. But we have made aggregate judgments by considering the diverse sources of information available.

In Houston, for example, the INS Investigations branch had virtually shut down its enforcement of sanctions in order to devote available resources to SAW fraud investigations. Houston's decision reflects a mix of considerations: a singular local commitment to investigating and prosecuting SAW applicants suspected of fraud, a severe budget crunch, and an abiding skepticism over the INS's ability to serve as a regulatory agency for U.S. business. As one senior official stated:

Sanctions is an albatross for the INS. It affects citizens more than aliens; and it should have been placed with the Department of Labor. The INS doesn't have the background in employer communities. We're juveniles in this thing.

Table 4.2   SITE ENFORCEMENT PRIORITIES: JUNE 1989

Site[a]	Priority
New York	criminal alien
El Paso	alien apprehension
Houston	SAWs fraud
Miami	criminal alien
San Antonio	criminal alien
Chicago	employer sanctions
Los Angeles	employer sanctions

a. Refers only to INS district offices.

Exercise of Caution

While district offices differed in the priority assigned sanctions, there was general agreement over the need for enforcement to proceed cautiously and to some extent deferentially with regard to the business community. Officials frequently noted to us that arbitrary, high-profile enforcement of the law could lead to a congressional sunset of the sanctions provisions. The near constant presence of auditors from the GAO further emphasized the need for INS staff to consider the fairness and legitimacy of the enforcement approach.

The incentives for INS managers and agents to implement the law in a cautious and creditable manner stemmed from more than sanctions' value as a potentially powerful tool for deterring illegal immigration. As one INS attorney stated, "If sanctions is sunset, we lose jobs and money. The incentive here is not just idealistic."

In some jurisdictions these concerns with legitimacy had a powerful impact on sanctions enforcement. This was felt most strongly in Chicago, where members of the immigration bar, who had been long-standing antagonists of the INS, noted the INS's businesslike approach to sanctions enforcement. When first interviewed, immigration bar members characterized the INS agents as "an instant-gratification crew" that would wreak havoc when turned loose on sanctions enforcement. But by the time of the second wave of interviews, their assessment had shifted. In the words of one attorney, "The attitude and the way we were able to control disruption (during an I-9 inspection) was 180 degrees different from anything we'd ever seen."

While this was the predominant response of immigration attorneys and employers interviewed, it was not the universal view. For example, others noted, "They used to have a hammer. Now they have a sledge hammer." And, "They [INS agents] used to be cowboys chasing people. Now they're cowboys chasing paper."

Other immigration attorneys simply were waiting for intensive enforcement to begin. "The human rights community is interested in how sanctions is being enforced, but there isn't enough activity for us to get involved."

Despite Agency-wide interest in preserving sanctions during the three-year probation period during which its implementation and outcomes would be under close GAO scrutiny, divergent approaches to enforcement were adopted in different cities. This diversity is reflected in strategies for targeting employers, investigations, and penalizing violators.

Targeting Employers for Investigation

At the local level, we observed the tensions that exist between achieving legitimacy goals (through the use of such tools as neutral targeting strategies) and the goal of generating impressive enforcement statistics. We also observed the INS's difficulties in expanding its enforcement effort by deputizing the DOL's Wage and Hour (W&H) inspectors.

Use of the General Administrative Plan (GAP). Random, neutral targeting has been broadly adopted if not accepted. All the local INS agencies we visited except one were implementing the GAP as well as the Special Emphasis Plan (SEP).[12]

While most of the agencies were meeting their GAP quotas, many reported that the share of staff time devoted to GAP cases was closer to 25 percent than to the 40 percent anticipated by INS central office planners. Some local offices purposely limited GAP inspections because they appeared unproductive. Few GAP inspections identified violations that led to enforcement actions,[13] and many targeted extremely small employers who rarely hired anyone (e.g., the frequently cited dentist with his lifelong secretary/technician). In other cases, officials believed that it was enough to advertise the existence of an inspection program and that it was unnecessary to devote major resources to it.

These views reflect a widespread skepticism among local INS staff about GAP's importance and cost-effectiveness. In Chicago, agents informed us that they counted calls to closed businesses as completed GAP visits. In Los Angeles, GAP visits were used to train inexperienced staff, and in San Antonio, Border Patrol agents were not doing GAP inspections at all.

A minority of our respondents valued random targeting as a means of avoiding charges of selective enforcement, identifying trends in noncompliance, and alerting employers in all industries that they must comply with IRCA. One New York official stated, "If all we did was lead-driven inspections, a whole segment of industry would never see immigration inspectors."

The approaches to identifying firms for SEP investigations also varied across sites. New York officials had no data sources identifying local industries that hired undocumented immigrants in the past; as a result, they limited SEP inspections to the garment industry. In Chicago, the SEP targeted a wide range of industries: landscapers, food preparers, hotels and motels, and construction. El Paso selected firms for SEP inspections by reviewing records of pre-IRCA contacts with firms employing undocumented aliens.

Labor Certifications. Some INS district offices were using DOL records of petitions for labor certification as key elements of their targeting strategy. These petitions, filed by employers, ask permission to hire an alien worker for a hard-to-fill specialist position. In theory, these positions are empty because qualified U.S. residents cannot be found to fill them and the requested alien employee will enter the U.S. only after certification is granted. In fact, many such workers are in the U.S. illegally and working for the employer at the time certification is requested. When the INS receives a petition, it may target the employer for investigation, suspecting that the immigrant is already working for the employer filing the petition.

If the agent's suspicion is borne out, the existence of a petition virtually proves the government's contention of a knowing hire. The simplicity of the resulting enforcement

Table 4.3   USE OF LABOR CERTIFICATES TO TARGET
ENFORCEMENT: JUNE 1989

Site[a]	Priority
New York	No
El Paso	Yes
Houston	Yes
Miami	Yes
San Antonio	Planned
Chicago	No
Los Angeles	Yes

a. Refers only to INS district offices.

action is attractive for INS offices that have limited investigative resources but need to generate a designated number of enforcement actions. In Miami, for example, labor certificate applications have been among that district's chief targeting methods, a development stemming from the high priority given to drug-related crime and the corresponding need to conserve enforcement resources. Table 4.3 identifies the INS districts that targeted employers on the basis of labor certification petitions.

Some immigration attorneys claim that the process has the look and feel of entrapment and that it harms employers making good-faith efforts to comply with the law. Some claim that it violates the employer's and the alien's constitutional rights to due process and protection from self-incrimination.

DOL Referrals. Referrals based on DOL Wage and Hour inspectors' reviews of I-9 forms are routinely received at INS offices. In many cases, however, they help expand an already large backlog of leads, tips, and complaints. DOL referrals are virtually ignored in some INS offices. As one agent stated, "DOL picks up paperwork violations, and we don't do paperwork violations." In Houston, for example, when the district office receives a report of apparent or clear I-9 noncompliance from DOL, investigators follow up with a letter to the suspected employer informing him or her of IRCA's requirements and the fact that the business has been identified as a possible violator. According to enforcement staff, there is no follow-up even if there is no response, a result that is attributed to budget constraints. Of our eight sites, DOL referrals appeared to be regularly pursued only in El Paso and Los Angeles.

Investigations

As with targeting, there was a sharp division among local INS offices in how they carried out sanctions investigations. Some followed a regulatory model. They approached enforcement as a regulatory function and emphasized the use of records in the development of a case. In other instances, the enforcement process was more focused on the apprehension of undocumented workers, relied more heavily on raids and street arrests, and used traditional INS enforcement techniques.

Initiation. The sites differed in the way an investigation was triggered. According to the nationally prescribed regulatory model, explained in chapter 2, employers to be investigated are identified through the GAP, through complaints or through DOL referrals. That is the case in New York, Chicago, and Los Angeles. Other methods are often used in sites closer to the border, with many leads coming from INS-initiated street encounters with aliens or apprehensions. As one Border Patrol respondent stated:

> Every employer we've developed a case on has been
> identified by an alien we already had in custody
> through our patrol efforts or had been turned over to
> us by the police.

In fact, in one Border Patrol office it was standard operating procedure for the agents to spend their mornings
apprehending aliens and their afternoons pursuing
enforcement actions against those aliens' employers. In
sum, we observed substantial variation in the degree to
which IRCA has led the INS to abandon an alien-focused
police model that depends on stops and arrests in favor of
the new employer-focused regulatory model that depends
on investigation and documents.

Dealing with the Employer. Once agents have made
contact with the employer, INS offices adopt one of two
strategies. Under the regulatory model, the INS makes
several visits to a work site, starting with an education
visit and proceeding through a careful review of the
employer's I-9s. Raids or fines come only after the
employer has had notice of his deficiencies and has been
given opportunities to resolve them.

By contrast, the police model that is in place in other
jurisdictions (and appears especially prevalent on the
border) is typically conducted in a more summary fashion.
A tip or apprehension leads to a raid rather than an education visit or an I-9 inspection. The I-9s are reviewed only
after the apprehension of undocumented aliens, and do
not serve as the engine of the enforcement process but
simply as an additional piece of evidence to be marshaled
against the employer. Under this model, enforcement
looks less like a regulatory law enforcement proceeding
than like an old-style INS raid involving entry, arrest, and
deportation.

INS offices in cities near the Mexican border were the most likely to rely on the police model. In El Paso, for example, a lead is received and followed by surveillance of the business and, in turn, a raid. Only following a raid and the apprehension of undocumented aliens is a three-day notice of inspection typically provided the employer. With minor variations, this sequence of events also resembles the enforcement process described to us by the Houston District Office.

The enforcement approach taken by both the San Antonio Border Patrol and Investigations staff starts with a tip and is followed by surveillance and then alien apprehension and deportation. After all this has transpired, the I-9 inspection process begins. The announced preference of the local enforcement staff is not to conduct a raid but to apprehend the aliens "after they leave the job site, where we don't need probable cause."

In Chicago, New York, and Los Angeles, the process conforms more closely to the compliance model. In New York, for example, an investigation starts with an education visit. Observations made during the course of an education visit may lead the agent to schedule an inspection to review the employer's I-9s. Following review of the I-9s, a notice of results of inspection letter is sent or delivered. A follow-up inspection is then made and if the employer has remained out of compliance with the law, he will be served with a NIF. On the face of it, this is a rather forgiving process because it provides the employer with at least three opportunities to "get the hint" and come into compliance.

But even this rather liberal path can be a barbed one. For example, education visits are not always conducted exclusively for the employer's edification. Some INS offices have treated education as the immediate precursor to enforcement, saying "When we find an employer with an illegal alien, first we educate him, and then we return three days later to seize his records and pick up any illegal aliens he has on site." Or, as another enforcement official stated, "When we make an appointment for an education visit, we don't tell them that we are going to be setting them up. If we did, they would go on an Oliver North shredding party."

Different INS branches in the same city (i.e., the Border Patrol and Investigations) can take different approaches to enforcement. This is partly due to different enforcement styles and coordination problems. For example, in Miami, San Antonio, and Houston, Border Patrol and Investigations enforcement efforts were not coordinated; that is, there was no rational division of the territory and no systematic referral process for leads, much less common targeting, fine, or settlement standards. Moreover, relations between enforcement staffs seemed antagonistic at times. In one site, for example, despite the existence of a memorandum of understanding assigning the Border Patrol lead enforcement responsibility in rural areas and Investigations the lead in urban areas, Investigations staff complained that the Border Patrol "was walking all over Investigations agents here."

As one district office supervisor in another city said,

> We're beside ourself about the Border Patrol presence [in the city]. . . . We want a good relationship with the employers. . . . They [the Border Patrol] aren't used to attorneys or the Fourth Amendment or any kind of restraints.

Another, concerned about the possibility that employers would complain about double jeopardy, said, "I'm worried we're going to get gangbanging complaints. . . . If we got overzealous, we could screw up the law."

Focus on Alien Apprehension. Our eight sites also varied in whether the primary focus of enforcement was on changing the employer's hiring practices or apprehending aliens.

The INS Chicago District Office has focused its effort on employers. Unauthorized alien workers were not apprehended when they were found in the work place. Instead, the employer was given notice of the fact that he was employing unauthorized aliens, and the workers were given voluntary departure notices while the inspectors were on the job site. The burden of firing the workers then fell to the employer, who knew that an INS agent would soon return to check to see if they continued to be employed. According to one senior district official, undocumented immigrants were not "apprehended or removed--they are simply dislocated."

A similar approach was noted in San Antonio, where one official stated:

> I don't care about the disposition of the illegal alien employee. Give him an I-210 [voluntary departure] and send him on his way. If you can give him employment authorization in exchange for his help-ing with the enforcement of your sanctions case, fine.

Other sites had still not adopted an employer focus. In Houston, for example, the investigations process typically began with a raid. Statements were taken from those apprehended, and aliens were deported unless they were also involved in a criminal matter. In several cities, the INS was committed to apprehending aliens and removing them from the country. As one supervisory agent said:

> We're not going to pick up an alien knowing that we're going to have to turn him loose. We're mandated by IRCA not just to enforce sanctions but to remove aliens from the U.S. If we do that, we feel like we're opening up jobs. We won't leave an

undocumented alien on the job, because they go from
one job to another.

Los Angeles initially adopted an employer focus for its
investigations, but our interviews in summer 1989 suggest
that some features of an alien-focused approach were
being adopted. District officials stated that they planned
to target prosecutions against undocumented immigrants,
charging those who had given employers fraudulent
documents with felonious false attestation. The INS would
reduce the charge to a misdemeanor, but the alien would
be deported and placed on notice that he would be prosecuted for a felony upon reentry. The program would be
widely publicized and used as a way to discourage
unauthorized aliens from seeking employment.

PENALTIES

Criminal Prosecutions of Employers

As chapter 2 explains, IRCA supplements the INS's civil
enforcement powers by providing for the criminal prosecution of employers. The grounds for such prosecutions
are two: a pattern and practice of knowingly hiring
unauthorized aliens, and intentionally harboring and
transporting undocumented immigrants.

One INS official enthusiastically described the useful-
ness of the harboring provisions in the following terms:

> We will emphasize the harboring provisions of IRCA.
> It is a beautiful statute and the best result of the law.
> It is a sleeper; it's wonderful. We can indict on
> harboring and seize the vehicle. We can cut the

> administrative stuff and go right to jail. It will have a
> major effect on enforcement. We don't have to
> educate employers about harboring the way we do
> about sanctions.

Despite this enthusiasm and the latent power of the criminal provisions, only half the INS offices in our eight sites claimed to have brought any criminal sanctions cases (see table 4.4).

The most vigorous use of criminal sanctions has been in San Antonio. The first four criminal prosecutions against employers took place during the citation period that ran from June 1, 1987 to June 1, 1988. According to local staff, criminal actions were brought against employers as a way of getting around constraints on civil sanctions during this period.

By our second wave of fieldwork in summer 1989, the San Antonio District's Investigations Office had seized over 50 automobiles and brought criminal charges against the four employers mentioned above. San Antonio may, however, be moving away from use of criminal sanctions. Local INS officials informed us that the district was no longer seizing vehicles because the U.S. Attorney did not want to prosecute violators, in part because requirements of the 1988 Anti-Drug Abuse Act complicate the seizures. Furthermore, we were told that both INS regional and central offices applied pressure on the district to start making civil sanctions cases and to abandon the criminal-focused efforts.

There have been other inhibitions to the broad use of criminal sanctions. The most powerful has been the resistance of U.S. attorneys. Respondents in New York, Miami, Chicago, Los Angeles and San Antonio all reported that U.S. attorneys had rejected criminal cases presented to them. While U.S. attorneys might be promoting the legitimacy of sanctions enforcement by rejecting poorly pre-

Table 4.4   CRIMINAL PROSECUTIONS UNDER IRCA (by
August 1989)

	Number of Criminal Cases	Type of Case
New York	0	
El Paso District	0	
El Paso Border Patrol		
Houston	1	Har & Trans[a]
Miami District	0	
Miami Border Patrol	0	
San Antonio District	4	Har & Trans
San Antonio Border Patrol	2	Har & Trans
Chicago	6	Har & Trans
Los Angeles	1	Pat & Prac[b]

a. Harboring and transporting.
b. Pattern and practice.

pared or politically questionable cases, it is likely that their rejection of these cases reflects the fact that their calendars are filled with more pressing criminal matters, such as high-profile drug or organized crime cases.

Other factors inhibiting the use of criminal sanctions are the inexperience of INS enforcement staff and the fact that criminal cases are expensive to prosecute.

Most criminal prosecutions that did take place relied on IRCA's harboring and transporting provisions, as employers were rarely charged with pattern and practice violations. This is probably due to the newness of the law and the fact that INS investigators seldom conduct follow-up investigations of employers cited for violations.[14]

To date, no strong national policy has emerged regarding criminal prosecutions of employers. As we see above, criminal sanctions--most notably harboring and transporting--were used to circumvent the constraints placed on enforcement during the sanctions citation period. Indeed, the appeal of criminal sanctions to enforcement personnel is based on the fact that they do not require such procedural niceties as a previous educational visit, a three-day inspection notice, or review of I-9 forms to make a case against an employer.

While the future of criminal sanctions under IRCA is unclear, two developments may encourage their use. A recent federal court decision reinforced the INS's authority to seize the vehicles of employers who have driven known undocumented aliens to work.[15] Furthermore, internal INS documents make clear that at least the Eastern and Northern regions have encouraged criminal law actions against employers by setting numerical goals for criminal prosecutions.

Civil Penalties

The usual penalties IRCA was expected to generate were civil fines. National and local INS offices have accordingly built their processes of investigation and penalty determination around civil actions. After analyzing data about civil penalty actions in our eight sites and on a national basis we found that:

- The INS has proposed a very small number of civil fines, relative both to the numbers of establishments covered by employer sanctions and to the number of investigations conducted;

- Patterns of civil penalties vary widely among INS regions and from district to district within regions in terms of the numbers of fines proposed, the aggregate amounts of fines imposed, the average size of fines, the proportions of fines that cite knowing substantive violations (relative to the proportion that cite only paperwork violations), and the numbers of fines per investigative person-year;

• Regional differences are due in part to the different enforcement problems encountered in different parts of the country and in part to regional and local differences in policy and procedure.

Average Fine Amounts. The average fine proposed against alleged violators varied widely across INS districts and Border Patrol sectors (see table 4.5). The lowest average NIF was $850 for the San Antonio District Office, and the highest average was $45,545 for the Chicago District Office.

The highest average fines in our sample of sites were assessed by the Northern and Eastern regions; based on nationwide data, nine out of the ten INS offices assessing the highest average fines are in those regions (see table 4.6). Average NIFs through March 1989 were $9,459 for the Northern Region, $8,176 for the Eastern, $3,942 for the Western, and $2,060 for the Southern Region.

Differences within regions are comparably striking. Within the Northern Region, for example, the average fines for major cities range from $45,545 in Chicago to $1,333 in Cleveland. This difference in the amount of NIFs reflects differences in strategy. At one level, it reveals a district office policy of reserving penalties for bad actors who have committed major violations, rather than pursuing enforcement against employers whose violations have been less egregious. At another level, however, it reveals differences in the mechanics of negotiating and reporting fines. Cleveland negotiates final fine amounts before it issues a NIF. In Chicago, the district office sets its NIFs at high levels and then negotiates them down. A recent review by the GAO of 300 sanctions cases brought by different INS offices showed that overall the Agency reduces the amount of the initial fine by an average of 59 percent.

Even within one city, there can be major differences in fines proposed by the INS district office and by the Border Patrol. In El Paso, for example, where the Border Patrol and the district office Investigations staff work together more closely than in any of the other sites we examined, average NIFs assessed were $3,900 for the Border Patrol and $6,645 for Investigations. This 70 percent difference pales in comparison to the nearly fourfold difference between the San Antonio District Office ($2,983) and the Laredo Border Patrol sector ($852), which covers much the same area.

Paperwork-Only Violations. We saw substantial variation across the country in the willingness of local INS enforcement offices to fine employers for technical, paperwork-only violations. In most sites, the majority of NIFs were based on substantive, knowing violations. But Los Angeles and El Paso emphasized paperwork violations (see table 4.7).[16] Los Angeles is an exceptionally important district, since it has the highest number of immigrants, immigrant-dependent employers, and enforcement agents of any city in the country.

These data reflect differences in local implementation. In Los Angeles, an employer's failure to verify the eligibility of a job applicant is considered grounds for a penalty; prosecution of paperwork violations is an element of Los Angeles's strategy for creating widespread voluntary compliance. One regional official said, "Verification is not a second-rate violation." Furthermore, regional NIF quotas and the fact that proposed fines

Table 4.5   AVERAGE FINES (as of March 31, 1989)

Site	No. of NIFs	NIFs/ 100,00 employers	Amount NIFs	Average NIFs
Chicago	11	6.1	$501,000	$45,545
New York	53	10.8	610,075	11,511
El Paso District	21	210.0	139,550	6,645
Miami	22	23.0	118,475	5,385
Los Angeles	67	20.6	298,700	4,458
Pembroke Pines BP	53	57.0	210,700	3,975
El Paso BP	99	990.0	386,130	3,900
Houston	53	67.1	204,850	3,865
Laredo BP	48	171.1	138,850	2,892
San Antonio	57	203.6	48,550	850

Table 4.6   TEN SITES WITH HIGHEST AVERAGE NIFs FOR NATION IN RANKING ORDER (as of March 31, 1989)

	Site	Region	No. of NIFS	Average NIF
1.	Chicago	Northern	11	$45,545
2.	Detroit BP	Northern	3	20,500
3.	Portland	Northern	17	20,444
4.	Omaha	Northern	10	15,795
5.	Washington	Eastern	6	13,667
6.	New York	Eastern	53	11,511
7.	Atlanta	Southern	31	9,823
8.	Spokane BP	Northern	8	9,744
9.	San Juan	Eastern	18	9,114
10.	Philadelphia	Eastern	21	9,002

Table 4.7   SHARE OF NIFs THAT DO NOT CITE A
            KNOWING VIOLATION (as of March 31, 1989)

Site	No. of NIFs	% Paperwork only	% Fines Paperwork only
Los Angeles	67	51	55
El Paso	21	43	59
Pem Pines BP	53	30	20
El Paso BP	21	23	12
New York	53	21	20
Laredo BP	48	15	5
San Antonio	57	12	16
Miami	22	5	5
Houston	53	2	0
Chicago	11	0	0

influence agents' salary and performance reviews encourage the citing of technical violations.

In Chicago, there is less weight placed on the quantity of violations cited and far more on bringing enforcement actions against major violators. Furthermore, there is a general district and regional policy against citing technical violations except in rare instances. Hence, it is not surprising that the INS's average fine in Chicago should be the highest in the nation (see table 4.6) and that during the period documented, it cited no paperwork-only violations. As one district official stated, "IRCA was about deterring illegal immigration, not filling out forms."

Again, regional data provide a good but imperfect predictor of the likelihood that a local enforcement office

Table 4.8 TEN LOCAL INS AGENCIES THAT CITE THE LARGEST PERCENTAGE OF PAPERWORK-ONLY VIOLATIONS[a] (as of March 31, 1989)

	Site	Region	No. of NIFS	% Paperwork only
1.	El Centro BP	Western	14	93
2.	New Orleans	Southern	189	93
3.	San Francisco	Western	49	86
4.	New Orleans BP	Southern	27	85
5.	Dallas	Southern	45	78
6.	Livermore	Western	28	75
7.	San Diego BP	Western	64	63
8.	Seattle	Northern	15	53
9.	Los Angeles	Western	67	51
10.	San Diego	Western	44	50

a. Includes only districts that have served more than 10 NIFs.

will cite paperwork-only violations. As table 4.8 indicates, most of the ten offices that cite the largest share of technical violations are in the Western and Southern regions.

The difficulty of proving a knowing violation may be driving local INS offices to cite only paperwork violations even when an unauthorized worker is apprehended. In New York, for example, we were told, "In the future, it may be that in lieu of making a knowing case, we may go for paperwork violations because they are easier." That same district's officials claimed that unauthorized aliens were removed from eight of the ten work sites of employers who were charged only with paperwork violations.

Numbers of Fines. As the first column of table 4.5 shows, the number of fines served in our sites was not large relative to the number of employers covered by IRCA. The number of NIFs approached 100 only for the El Paso Border Patrol by March 31, 1989.

The numbers of fines served also varied by region. Of the ten local INS offices with highest numbers of NIFs served as of March 31, 1989, nine are in the Southern and the Western regions (see table 4.9).

The difference in enforcement staff size cannot account for regional differences in numbers of fines proposed. Agents in the Southern and Western regions propose more fines per person-year than agents in the Northern and Eastern regions. The El Paso Border Patrol issues 5.3 NIFs per agent year, roughly ten times the number issued by the Investigations staff of the Chicago District Office. Yet the amount of fines assessed per agent-year by the two organizations remains roughly the same: $23,000 (El Paso Border Patrol) vs. $25,000 (Chicago District Office).

Plainly, we are capturing differing strategies of enforcement--assessing large fines against a few egregious violators vs. smaller fines against larger numbers of employers. In Chicago, for example, we were told "You're not going to find numbers in this district; you're going to find quality." In contrast, a Western regional official described the general enforcement approach taken in the Southern and Western regions in this way: "In the Western Region and in Texas, we need to touch as many people as possible to let them know we're serious."

These differences may reflect adaptations to the enforcement problems faced by the different regions. Undocumented immigrants comprise a large proportion of the labor force of many western and southern cities, and they work in a large range of industries. Many of their employers are themselves immigrant entrepreneurs on the margins of the economy. Enforcement officials in the

Table 4.9   TEN LOCAL AGENCIES SERVING THE LARGEST
NUMBER OF NIFs (as of March 31, 1989)

	Site	Region	No. of NIFS
1.	New Orleans	Southern	189
2.	El Paso BP	Southern	99
3.	McAllen BP	Southern	81
4.	Harlingen	Southern	71
5.	Los Angeles	Western	67
6.	San Diego BP	Western	64
7.	San Antonio	Southern	57
8.	New York	Eastern	53
9.	Pembroke Pines BP	Southern	53
10.	Houston	Southern	53

North and the East may operate on the assumption that immigrants in eastern and northern cities are less numerous and may be more concentrated.[17] Thus, to influence employers' hiring patterns, enforcers in the West and South may believe they need to create a widespread fear of enforcement, whereas enforcers in the East and North may seek to maximize their influence by imposing large penalties on representative members of the few immigrant-dependent industries.

Chicago's strategy at the beginning of sanctions implementation--pursuing only knowing hires and exacting large fines--may have increased the Agency's bargaining leverage. A large candy manufacturer, found to be employing over 400 undocumented workers, fired all unauthorized employees within two days of receiving notice of their status. No further enforcement action was needed or taken.

The number of fines is affected by quota systems established by individual regions and districts. Quotas, "targets," and "numerical thresholds" are facts of life in the INS. They are, in fact, the focus of the priorities management system, which sets numerical targets for sanctions activity at regional and local levels. As one senior administrator told us:

> They are written right into the work plans. Obviously, I disagree with that. The stats are written right into your performance evaluation. The ratings relate directly to pay. There are five ratings categories: unsuccessful, minimally successful, fully successful, very successful, and outstanding; and these depend directly on meeting your numbers.

In the Western Region, where some members of the immigration bar charged that quotas were supplemented with monetary bonuses for sanctions enforcement, we found that INS staff had issued large numbers of NIFs.

Such "productivity" incentives could discourage staff from making refined calculations of employers' bad faith or likely future compliance. This could threaten the legitimacy of the enforcement effort and undermine the Congress's express intent that:

> The Immigration and Naturalization Service . . . target its enforcement resources on repeat offenders and that the size of the employer shall be a factor in the allocation of such resources.[18]

On the other hand, relatively high numbers of fines do influence local employers' calculation of their own likelihood of being inspected or penalized.

Criteria to be used in setting fines are announced by INS regulation, which states that the size of the firm, the number and seriousness of the violations, the good faith of the defendant, and the employer's previous history of violations should be taken into account.[19] In the field, however, there appears to be room for improvisation. For example, in San Antonio, key enforcement personnel look to the following in gauging fines: whether the unauthorized employee is displacing a U.S. citizen, whether the employer was aware of IRCA, and what the prospects of future compliance on the part of the employer are. While these are clearly related to regulatory criteria, they are not the same.

Numbers of actions and the dollar amount of fines assessed also reflect the philosophies of the district and Border Patrol attorneys, who must sign every NIF. Our field interviews show how district counsel staff, particularly in Chicago and Houston, can influence enforcement. As one agent said:

> We write the cases up here, but 75 percent of the time we have hassles with the attorneys. We say they should go for the max--we know what the attitude (of the employer) is. The attorney hasn't been lied to or cheated. But he says mitigate it down.

Finally, it bears repeating that during the period covered by our study--June 1, 1988 through June 1, 1989--the number of enforcement actions taken against employers across the country was generally low. Even in El Paso, where NIFs were most frequently served, the Border Patrol issued one fine for every two months of agent service. In Chicago, that rate fell to one NIF for every two years of agent service. Plainly, INS enforcement activity during this period cannot be characterized as hyperactive, despite regional quotas and other staff incentives for high numbers of proposed fines.

Employer Targets of Enforcement. Again, we saw substantial variation among the eight sites. In New York,

Los Angeles, and especially in Chicago, employers charged with violations came from many different industries. They included a proportionate share of large, formally organized and well-financed companies. In the other sites, virtually all enforcement actions were against small, ethnic-owned businesses.

This targeting of enforcement has meant that many firms cited for violations are small businesses that lack the legal and organizational resources needed to fight government enforcement actions. At the same time, however, they may be the most likely to hire undocumented workers. A large share of the defendants in these cases are ethnic restaurant owners. Indeed, some Agency officials thought the prevalence of enforcement actions against these businesses in some districts was so great as to raise the possibility of lawsuits for selective enforcement.

In sum, the patterns of IRCA penalties suggests that there are two regional models of enforcement. The Eastern and Northern regions emphasize small numbers of large fines based on substantive violations. The Southern and Western regions emphasize larger numbers of small fines, many based on technical violations rather than knowing hires of undocumented aliens. As noted above, some differences in enforcement strategy may reflect thoughtful responses to differences in the size and dispersion of the alien population and in the numbers of firms likely to employ undocumented aliens. However, the sharp regional variations and the emphasis on paperwork fines in some places raise questions about the consistency and fairness of sanctions' implementation. As one Western Region official stated, "I have seen no evidence to counter the criticism that the fines are low, and it's just a paper chase. We go for the letter, not the spirit, of the law." Or, as one district official in a Western city said, "Sensible targeting is not done: everyone is geared up to meet NIF quotas. We go after little, certain cases. It's like shooting fish in a barrel."

SUMMARY

Approaches to implementation vary widely in our sites in terms of whether the local enforcement process involves conducting multiple visits to give employers an opportunity to come into compliance versus taking a more summary and often punitive approach; whether aliens or employers serve as primary enforcement targets; and the degree to which criminal penalties are pursued against employers who have hired unauthorized workers. At the same time, penalties for violators varied in terms of the size of fines assessed, the character of violations singled out for punishment, i.e., the emphasis placed on technical vs. substantive violations, the number of fines issued, and the targets of sanctions.

Divergent implementation practices may be partially explained by the fact that the INS has assigned responsibility to two largely independent branches-- Inspections and the Border Patrol--and because of the INS's tradition of decentralized policymaking at the region and district levels. Variation also results from limited central oversight. As this report was being compiled, the central office did not have a way to get access electronically to data that would permit officials to monitor whether similar cases were being dealt with in a similar manner across the country. Furthermore, given the traditional autonomy of the regions and districts, nominal national policies (e.g., that paperwork-only violations be "egregious") were often subject to widely different interpretation in the field. Indeed, the national office did not conduct the kind of rigorous oversight of sanctions implementation adopted by the Eastern regional office. There, a standing panel of attorneys and officials reviews all proposed enforcement actions to ensure their consistency with regional and national policy.

The strength of local leadership also drives variation. Some local officials took a strong position in shaping enforcement. In Chicago, for example, local INS leaders articulated a clear enforcement strategy, consistent with the regulatory model described above, that appears to have been internalized by the enforcement staff. In sites where local leaders took a more hands-off approach, decisionmaking fell to field staff. In those places, implementation emphasized traditional enforcement approaches and targets.

In a few areas, however, we noted important ways in which local enforcement practices appeared to converge. Neutral targeting strategies have been broadly adopted (although the share of manpower dedicated to them differs, as does the level of commitment to their success), and district and sector counsel exert considerable authority in the enforcement process, making a final determination of the legality of all NIFs. Finally, two possible enforcement tactics were absent. There has been a general abandonment of mass apprehensions as a strategy of immigration law enforcement and, with one exception, households have been excluded from the focus of sanctions enforcement.

Notes, chapter four

1. U.S. Bureau of the Census, County Business Patterns, 1986, Selected States, U.S. Government Printing Office, Washington, D.C., 1988. See especially Table 2: Counties--Employees, Payroll and Establishments by Industry: 1986.

2. Cf. Executive Order 85-1, Office of Chicago Mayor Harold Washington, March 7, 1985; New York City Executive Order

1245, August 7, 1989. The City of Los Angeles has recently implemented an employment program that purposefully makes available employment opportunities to undocumented residents. See *New York Times*, October 26, 1989, p. A1.

3. See The City of New York, et al., v. U.S. Department of Commerce, et al. 88 Civ. 3474 (JMcL).

4. For example, the Mexican American Legal Defense and Education Fund filed an amicus brief on behalf of the employer in USA v. New El Rey Sausage Company, U.S. Department of Justice, Executive Office for Immigration Review, Office of the Chief Administrative Hearing Officer, Case No. 88100080.

5. See Almeida-Sanchez v. U.S. 413 U.S. 266 (1973), holding that neither probable cause nor reasonable suspicion is required for general searches at the border or the functional equivalent of the border.

6. The INS was itself an advocate for the Moorhead Amendment, which called for an "increase in the border patrol personnel of the Immigration and Nationalization Service so that the average level of such personnel in each of fiscal years 1987 and 1988 is at least 50 percent higher than such level for FY 1986." See 8 USC 1101.

7. The criminal alien sections of district Investigations offices typically address narcotics cases involving immigrants and deportation of convicted criminals from state, local, and federal prisons.

8. OCDETF commits a share of Investigations staff to participation in an interagency drug enforcement task force that is directed by the Justice Department.

9. The fraud sections of district Investigations offices address legalization-related fraud, public benefit fraud, marriage fraud, and the manufacture and distribution of fraudulent documents.

10. Turnover in Border Patrol agents assigned to sanctions duty appears to be due, in part, to union concerns, which do not allow field agents to remain in sanctions enforcement for more than 12 months.

11. According to federal estimates, the Agency was about $50 million over its budget at one point because of the policy. In Texas, the Door to Central Americans Opens a Crack, *New York Times*, January 28, 1990, p. E-4.

12. See discussion of targeting above, p. 57.

13. The only exception was in El Paso, where 10 percent of GAP inspections led to enforcement actions.

14. However, a limited number of pattern and practice prosecutions that did not build on prior successful prosecutions under IRCA have been brought to court. One, United States of America v. DAVCO Food, Inc., was filed in federal court in the Eastern District of Alexandria in July, 1988. The complaint charged the defendant with 13 cases of knowing hire and/or continuing employment violations from November 6, 1986 through May 31, 1988. Significantly, the suit was not the result of the accumulation of separately cited violations over time.

15. United States v. One 1984 Ford Pickup Truck __ F. Supp. __, CA 3-88-2291-R (N.D. Tex. August 30, 1989). See Judge Upholds INS Vehicle Seizure for Transporting Undocumented Alien, *Interpreter Releases*. Sept. 18, 1989, p. 1033.

16. The number of complaints that cite only paperwork violations is an imperfect gauge of the share of identified violations that are technical alone--i.e., where no undocumented aliens are found to be working on the premises but where the employer has failed to fill out I-9s or has filled them out improperly. In some instances, the NIF may cite only paperwork violations because the challenges of proving a substantive violation, e.g., a knowing hire, are unlikely to be met. In those cases, the Agency may include only paperwork violations in the

NIF. In short, these figures tend to overstate paperwork-only violations.

17. See B. Chiswick, *Illegal Aliens, Their Employment and Employers*, Kalamazoo, Michigan, W. E. Upjohn, 1988, which finds that undocumented immigrants in Chicago are widely distributed across the spectrum of low-wage industries despite pockets of concentration in selected industries.

18. Conference Report No. 99-1000, 99th Cong. 2nd Sess. 86.

19. 52 F.R. 16225, Sec. 274a.10(b)(2), May 2, 1987.

Chapter Five

EMPLOYER PERSPECTIVES
ON IMPLEMENTATION

One of IRCA's central policy innovations was assigning
responsibility for verifying employment authorization to
employers, who are called upon to act as "junior
immigration inspectors."[1] To understand their role in the
law's implementation, and the effects of INS actions on
them, we conducted a total of 184 employer interviews,
half from November to December 1988 and half from June
to July 1989. The GAO has completed surveys nationally
representative of all employers, so we did not try to
duplicate their work. We focused instead on employers in
immigrant-dependent industries whose hiring practices
were most likely to be altered by IRCA, and who were
likely to come into contact with the INS implementers. We
concentrated our interviews, which were conducted by
phone and in person, on firms in the restaurant,
construction, light manufacturing, and janitorial and clean-
ing industries. To provide a comparison with "mainstream" nonimmigrant-dependent employers, we also
interviewed representatives of large financial and
manufacturing firms.

Like our other interviews, these were designed to
explore the respondent's attitudes and strategies rather
than to collect quantitative data. While we did probe for
concrete facts and figures, our principal aim was to
understand 1) the scope and character of INS imple-

mentation activities as experienced by employers, 2) the extent of these employers' awareness of and efforts to comply with IRCA's requirements, 3) the costs that businesses have incurred and the practices that they have been forced to alter in response to IRCA, and 4) the impact of these new practices on foreign-sounding and foreign-looking job applicants.

While we made every effort to draw an unbiased sample, we had difficulty obtaining employer responses. When faced with a request to discuss the sensitive subject of a firm's hiring practices, many firms turned our interviewers down. In some industries, the refusal rate was as high as 15:1. The sample, then, is probably biased toward respondents who are not afraid to talk about their hiring policies. We would expect that bias to mean that our respondents are somewhat more informed about IRCA.

Among our respondents we found the following trends:

- Those firms that have been the target of INS educational or investigative activities report that these activities are not disruptive or punitive in character;

- Most firms know about IRCA's ban on the hiring of undocumented workers, but many are not in full compliance with the record-keeping requirements;

- Knowledge of the law and the completeness of efforts to comply vary by industry and are generally best in firms that have formal personnel systems or are required by other regulatory or contractual requirements to document their hiring practices;

- Few firms report major changes in their labor costs, production methods, or other business practices;

- Though few respondents reported openly discriminating against foreign-looking or foreign-sounding applicants, many do not accept the full range of work eligibility documents permitted by the law. The exclusion of some legitimate documents could work to the disadvantage of foreign-born job applicants.

EMPLOYER PERCEPTIONS OF INS ACTIVITY

We tried to assess from the firms interviewed the extent and the character of INS enforcement activity. Had the government made its presence felt? Had it been able to reach employers to explain their new responsibilities? Where some contact had been made, how could it be characterized? Was it civil, useful, or disruptive?

Because we selected firms from traditionally immigrant-dependent industries, our respondents probably had a better-than-average chance of being targets of INS activity. We found that over 40 percent of respondents had personal contact with an INS agent, either before or after IRCA's enactment, with only a small majority pre-dating IRCA.[2] This high level of INS coverage was especially evident among respondents within El Paso, San Antonio, and Los Angeles, where 70 percent, 60 percent and 50 percent, respectively, of our respondents reported direct contact with Agency officers. These results reflect in part the fact that El Paso and San

Antonio house both INS district offices as well as INS Border Patrol offices. This level of INS activity led employers within these cities to expect to be inspected by INS in the coming year. One San Antonio construction manager stated, "I am complying because I do not want to get fined. I don't want my name in the media, at least not under those circumstances." A restaurant owner said: "I think I might have reason to anticipate a visit from the INS. I saw an ad in the paper about hiring new Border Patrol agents, 500 of them, just for I-9 enforcement. If they come, they come. I am all ready for them."

In our other sites, one-quarter to one-third of the respondents had direct contact with INS. Most of the firms that reported education and enforcement contacts were larger than average (with 50 or more employees). Few of the smaller employers reported an INS contact or expected one during the coming year.

Only one of the firms that had been contacted by the INS reported having been fined, and none reported that INS visits had proved especially disruptive.

> They audited us. They were real nice about it. They gave us three days' notice. They only checked the I-9s, they did not look at our payroll records.

> They did come and see if we were doing the I-9 forms. I don't know if they asked to see them or not, but I offered to show them the I-9s. We were doing it right, so I don't think they will be coming back unless they do a spot check or something.

In sum, it appears from our limited sample of firms that at least among larger firms in these immigrant-dependent industries, the INS's coverage has been rather broad. It also appears that its activities have focused on education and that respondents did not perceive inspections of their premises to be especially disruptive or punitive in nature.

EMPLOYER AWARENESS AND COMPLIANCE EFFORTS

Most employers (90 percent) in our sample appeared aware of IRCA's ban on the hiring of undocumented labor, and a comparably large percentage claimed to be conducting some type of formal verification procedures in hiring. This high level of reported compliance substantially exceeds that reported by the DOL's Wage and Hour Division, which found that only 70 percent of firms visited in the course of its routine inspections were filling out the I-9 form required by IRCA.[3]

The accuracy of employers' understanding of the requirements of implementation varied enormously. Almost 40 percent of our respondents had a detailed understanding of the law's new verification requirements. They seemed unlikely to commit unwitting violations, even on minor technicalities. On the other hand, a roughly equivalent share of the respondents described their responsibilities in terms that were vague enough to raise the possibility that they might commit violations while trying to comply (e.g., by requiring documentation only of noncitizens, by accepting only certain identification documents, by asking applicants for documents at different stages in the hiring process).

Finally, approximately one in ten of the employers we interviewed displayed serious ignorance or misunderstanding of the law, as evidenced by these responses:

> We don't review documents of people who apply for jobs. I haven't done anything to comply with the law. I guess you could say that we're fat, dumb, and happy and not concerned about it.

> I know that you can't hire illegal aliens, but that's always been the law . . . . I've never heard of the I-9 form.

> The only thing that we're supposed to check is that we're not employing illegal aliens, I guess. It's truthfully something that we don't pay that much attention to. You mean to tell me there's a form we're supposed to fill out on every employee? I'm sure it's not happening.

Only one in twenty respondents claimed that they did not inspect job candidates' documents. (Again, this is a lower rate than reported by the DOL, which found that six in twenty firms did not have I-9 records on file for employees.) Furthermore, it appeared that compliance increased over time. Between our first and second waves of fieldwork, we noted an increase in both the number of respondents who required documents and in the number who knew which documents could be accepted.

Changes in Hiring Practices

Despite our best efforts, employers were on their guard during our interviews and were therefore unlikely to admit continuing to hire undocumented workers. However, nearly 60 percent believed that their firms had hired illegal workers before November 1, 1986. Furthermore, nearly 30 percent said they had helped employees apply for amnesty. One in five said they had dismissed undocumented workers after IRCA sanctions began in 1988. It appears, then, that the law dictated some form of behavioral adjustment on the part of many of the firms within our sample.

Understanding of the law's requirements and efforts to bring hiring practices into line were most clearly evident in larger firms with central office staff units dedicated to personnel and record-keeping functions. Changed practices were also evident in small branches or franchises of larger firms that normally relied on the parent organization and personnel services. When specialization occurred--even if it only meant the firm employed a full-time bookkeeper or personnel officer--employers often displayed a comparatively detailed understanding of IRCA requirements, and had made document checking and completion of the I-9 form a routine part of the hiring process. The largest employers and branch offices had the advantage of corporate bureaucracies with specialized legal and personnel departments, which had thoroughly routinized IRCA paperwork.

Some employers in our sample, however, were anything but formally organized. One business was owned and operated by an individual who took telephone orders on his apartment phone and drove dress patterns and materials out to women who did sewing in their homes. Another business was a partnership between two brothers who repaired cars in a sand lot. Many such employers lack formal procedures of any kind, even for payroll and billing, and are therefore unlikely to incorporate new procedures at their own initiative. However, four out of five firms with fewer than 20 employees surveyed reported conducting formal verification procedures.

Firms that did business with government agencies or were overseen by regulatory agencies were likely to have taken all the actions required by IRCA. Bonding and hiring requirements set, for example, by the Federal Deposit Insurance Corporation (FDIC) may have as much to do with financial institutions' compliance with IRCA as does the law's verification requirements and penalty structure. Much the same was true of several janitorial services in our sample that worked under contract to federal agencies. From their managers' statements it was clear that compliance with federal requirements had become habitual, so that the response to IRCA was due as much to the prospects of random EEOC and contracting audits as to the specific enforcement of IRCA.

Though it is impossible to project from our sample to the economy as a whole, some of the response patterns we observed are probably representative of a larger national pool. For example, we observed different forms of compliance activity across types of firms. Financial service firms exhibited the most complete understanding of and compliance with the law. All reported that they conducted formal verification procedures and indicated that they requested all appropriate documents. Most had an administrator whose work was devoted to affirmative action and other personnel requirements. Respondents repeatedly reminded our interviewers that they were not the sort of firm that was traditionally dependent on an immigrant labor force. In contrast, construction firms showed the lowest level of understanding and response to IRCA. One in four of our respondents from that industry did not report having any verification procedure in place, and only one in five made clear that they accepted the full range of appropriate documents. Compliance levels across manufacturing and janitorial firms and restaurants were roughly comparable and, in general, fell between the poles represented by financial service and construction firms.

EMPLOYER COSTS AND CHANGED BUSINESS PRACTICES

We asked employers how IRCA has affected their business practices--whether they had more paperwork, more difficulty recruiting or retaining workers, were forced to pay higher wages or benefits, or had changed locations or production methods.

One-quarter of our respondents believed that IRCA had imposed additional costs on their operations. Costs are likely to be claimed by the largest firms (where compliance is likely to be the most complete) even though institutional structures (personnel departments, in-house counsel, etc.) should keep marginal costs low. The larger firms are more likely to report costs because they appear more able and inclined than smaller firms to identify and quantify the costs that flow from a new set of prescribed activities. Furthermore, their more "complete" compliance may impose additional costs.

Two primary types of compliance costs were identified: costs associated with paperwork and costs flowing from higher wages. While many respondents complained that completing the I-9 form was a burden, only 15 percent actually ascribed increased costs to it. In many cases, this was due to the difficulty of calculating these additional costs.

> [The only costs imposed are] in time and that's very hard to measure. When someone fills out the W-2, he or she fills out the I-9 too. So how do you measure that?

> There is more paperwork. This takes up more of my time, but the cost is absorbed in my salary.

Some firms complained that it was difficult for them to keep track of the expiration dates of their workers' provisional work authorization (their Temporary Resident Alien status, for example). They recognized that such employees might once again become illegal, subjecting their employers to enforcement action.

Approximately one in eight firms surveyed complained of having to pay higher wages as a result of IRCA. Large companies with over 100 employees accounted for the majority of firms with this complaint. Many of these firms ascribed increased wage costs to IRCA's amnesty program rather than to employer sanctions, as illustrated by these two responses:

> It [IRCA's amnesty program] has affected our costs. The number of people who would like to do this kind of job has declined. Before, illegal workers were afraid to move or to change jobs. Now they have a new freedom. Although we start people at $3.35, most of our workers are working for $5 per hour. We lost a few people, and then others threatened to quit unless we paid them more. We had to start paying them to keep them in our shop. Our prices have gone up somewhat, but not as much as the wages. We are absorbing the costs. It is eating into our profits.

> We dismissed the illegal aliens and raised the salaries of the dishwashers. Now we have a house for them. We went a month without decent help. We tried a private employment agency, but no one would come. The workers got more lazy--you can't talk to them now; you've got to kiss their feet. You gotta have meetings once in a while.

The vast majority of our respondents reported that recruiting entry-level employees was no more difficult than before IRCA. However, over one-third of those interviewed reported being unable to hire promising job applicants because they were unable to produce documents or they did not return after having been asked to provide documentation.

Only in Los Angeles did a significant proportion (one-third) of our respondents report having to cope with increased worker turnover. They attributed the turnover (and a less compliant attitude among workers) to legalization.

> It is hard to find real Mexican cooks. Once they get their amnesty they eat up and steal all our profits. They think they have it made. I've lost my whole staff--they've gone to work in American restaurants and clean hotels because they make more money. They say they are going to Mexico for 5 to 6 days, and they stay gone months.

A third type of cost was administrative compliance costs, e.g., the legal fees and other costs associated with establishing systems of records to demonstrate compliance. These costs were most frequently reported by large firms.

Few of our respondents reported significant changes in production methods, services offered, or the location of operations. One San Jose janitorial firm did, however, report exploring the feasibility of using robots. The prospects were not strong.

Employer Evasion Strategies

Few of our employers would admit taking steps to evade punishment under the sanctions law other than rejecting illegal alien job applicants. Several construction firms increased their use of outside contractors. Two other employers said that they had hired help through personal service contracts, hoping that workers would eventually find acceptable documentation so that they could be made regular employees. Two admitted filling positions on a daily basis, paying workers in cash at the end of each day, and inviting the best ones to return.

From our sample, however, it appears that employers' chief method of evasion is pro forma paper compliance.

Even those who know little about IRCA understand that they are better off accepting a questionable document and filling out an I-9 form than having a totally undocumented employee. Since some strange looking documents turn out to be valid (e.g., handwritten green cards issued by the INS in one city, or expired driver's licenses), employers have an incentive to accept documents and hope that a claim of good faith will protect them. As one employer stated, "I'm not going to become a document expert for the U.S. government."

However, others take upon themselves the responsibility of judging the authenticity of the documents they are presented. One such respondent stated, "We have to get proper documentation from each worker and make a judgment call as to whether or not we think that it is legitimate."

Employer Discrimination

Our survey could not measure discrimination directly. And though respondents told us of actions that may exclude eligible foreign-born workers from jobs, we could not tell whether those actions reflected employers' fear of INS enforcement or more deep-seated prejudices. Some employers clearly betrayed ethnic and citizenship biases, such as one respondent who stated, "I am lucky to have a group of guys who have a college education and are all-American and look like it. Everyone I hire is a true-blue American, a real flag waver."

But others praised foreign-born workers and condemned the incompetence, dishonesty, and poor work ethic of native-born workers. In other cases, employers' screening may technically violate IRCA's antidiscrimination rules without ultimately denying job opportunities to authorized workers. This was the case with one respondent, who told us, "I tell them on the phone that they will have to provide me with documents if there is any doubt in my mind, like they have an accent."

Most of the potentially discriminatory policies revealed in our interviews arose from incomplete understanding of IRCA's verification requirements. The most common failure was accepting only some of the admissible documents, usually a driver's license and a social security card. In some cases employers require foreign-looking and foreign-sounding applicants to produce different documentation than they require of others.

> We ask everyone for documents after we hire them and before they start to work. If they look like they could have been from Mexico, then we ask them for the Alien Registration card. If they have been here longer, then they probably have a driver's license and a Social Security card.

CONCLUSION

Delegating responsibility for enforcing sanctions to employers created a number of tensions. First, employers were expected to screen job applicants for eligibility, but were required to know and accept a wide variety of different documents. Second, employers could not "overcomply" with IRCA by employing higher standards of proof than the law required, because that might lead to the exclusion of eligible foreign-born workers.

As we have seen, most members of our sample seemed to be aware of the law and expressed no fervent desire to evade it. Many were, however, doing a spotty job of implementing worker verification and record-keeping requirements. Some of these shortcomings could work to the disadvantage of authorized but foreign-sounding and foreign-looking applicants subjected to close scrutiny and narrowly specified document requests.

Facilitating employee compliance will be a challenge for future IRCA implementers. Where law enforcement responsibility devolves on nonspecialist private citizens, procedures need to be as simple as possible (as years of citizen complaints over the complexity of tax forms has shown). A system that relies on unsophisticated implementers must present simple choices and provide all necessary information. For IRCA, this suggests the need to simplify employers' tasks as document inspectors. Education is a second-best strategy. It may convey the broad contours of a law, but it will rarely provide laymen with the detailed understanding necessary for complete compliance.

Small, loosely organized firms are a particular problem for IRCA implementation. Their understanding of the law is often deficient, as is their implementation of IRCA's verification procedures. As a result, they are more likely to commit both deliberate and inadvertent violations. In contrast, large, formally organized firms have generally adopted IRCA's verification procedures and are in substantial compliance with the law's sanctions and discrimination requirements. Consequently, this segment of the economy is probably even less open to undocumented immigrants than it was prior to IRCA. But the vast population of small firms, including those that offer low wages and may depend on undocumented immigrants, still require help in the form of simpler compliance procedures, continued education, and a determined education and enforcement effort.

Notes, chapter five

This chapter was written with Julie Goldsmith of The Urban Institute.

1. On this point, see M. Roberts and S. Yale-Loehr, Employers as Junior Immigration Inspectors: The Impact on the 1986 Immigration Reform and Control Act, 21 International Lawyer 1013, 1987.

2. We interpreted "contact" to mean an investigation prior to IRCA and, following IRCA, an educational visit, an inspection visit, attendance at an INS seminar, or an employer-initiated call to the INS.

3. See "Employment Eligibility Verification (I-9) Inspection Summary," Employment Standards Administration, June 1, 1989. This discrepancy could be due to the fact that our respondents were largely self-selected, while DOL examinations are mandatory. It could also be due to the fact that because of their historical use of undocumented workers, the firms in our sample are more aware of IRCA's requirements than are those visited by the DOL.

Chapter Six

CONCLUSIONS

As this is being written, the story of sanctions implementation is far from complete. Enforcement in rural areas has just begun, and it will impose new problems for enforcement strategy and create new demands on the INS's limited investigative manpower. Key IRCA programs--SAW, RAW, and Phase II of the main legalization program--are still developing, and their full effects on the supply and distribution of labor are unknown. Growth in the enforcement budget has halted due to government-wide stringency. The future of the employer sanctions program itself could be threatened by evidence that it has stimulated "widespread discrimination" against authorized, but foreign-sounding or foreign-looking workers. The GAO spoke to this issue in March 1990, based at least in part on evidence assembled by The Urban Institute. Finally, the strategic approach to sanctions could shift if and when Congress decides not to "sunset" this provision.

Still, two forms of assessment are possible now. We can judge the progress of implementation to date in light of the challenges and constraints that faced the INS and other responsible agencies, and we can identify problems that must be faced in the future.

Our assessment of implementation takes into account several basic characteristics of the INS that have been discussed in this report. In the first place, prior to IRCA, the Agency had little experience directly regulating U.S. employers. Furthermore, over the years its enforcement branches had been chronically undermanned; the Agency had grown unusually decentralized; and it had historically been subject to criticism for the arbitrariness of its enforcement activity. All raised concerns about the legitimacy and effectiveness of enforcement, and tempered expectations.

PROGRESS TO DATE

Over the first three years, the INS made substantial progress toward meeting the implementation challenges posed by legitimacy, legality, organizational adaptation, and resource scarcity. At the national level, where general policies and practices were developed, and at the local and regional levels, where policies were put into operation and at times modified in application, IRCA's implementers made the following progress:

They headed off any fundamental challenge by the regulated community to the legitimacy of a potentially controversial and burdensome regulatory regime. Though individual employers have complained about local tactics, the larger employment community has not organized to oppose the policy or its implementation. To some extent, however, this lack of opposition has been accomplished by means of low levels of enforcement activity and by concentrating enforcement on disorganized and undercapitalized firms. While these firms were the most likely to employ illegal aliens, they would not prove strong opponents. Credit for the political success of sanctions implementation should be claimed in part by the Congress itself, which foresaw the need for a transition period and for extensive employer education. However, substantial confusion remains regarding compliance with the complex documentation requirements established by the law and, in general, education efforts regarding the law's nondiscrimination provisions have been inadequate.

IRCA's implementers generally operated within the boundaries of administrative law and procedure, which to a greater degree than immigration law emphasizes the rights of the regulated over the powers of the regulators. Though many unresolved legal issues remain, to date the INS has avoided legal reversals that would cripple future implementation. This success in court is in stark contrast to the Agency's record in the context of challenges to standards and practices regarding legalization. It reflects the INS General Counsel Office's early efforts to anticipate problems, standardize procedures, and require that lawyers authorize all NIFs. It may also reflect the avoidance of "hard" cases.

IRCA's implementers, especially INS officials in the largest cities, have begun the process of adapting the Agency's culture and operations to the exacting demands of a program that regulates U.S. citizens. However, this conversion from a paramilitary and police agency to one that is also a regulatory and educational organization is still incomplete, as traditional targeting and enforcement approaches have been retained in many local agencies, most notably those within border communities.

IRCA's implementers have made progress in adapting to the vast scope of a regulatory program that covers all U.S. employers, finding ways to inform millions of employers about their obligations, and creating a broad awareness of the existence of the new law. The INS in particular has succeeded in expanding the size and capability of the staff responsible for employer sanctions implementation. Though hiring has been slowed by budget crises and manpower has often been diverted to other tasks, in general, recruits to enforcement and legal positions have been of high quality, and the INS's enforcement capability has increased over the past three years.

Thus, despite the exceptions noted earlier, our main conclusion stands: During the first three years of employer sanctions, the INS made substantial progress toward meeting the implementation challenges that face it.

FUTURE ISSUES AND POTENTIAL PROBLEMS

The question remains whether current implementation arrangements are a good foundation for the future. If implementation proceeds along currently established lines, will it continue meeting the challenges of legitimacy, legality, organizational adaptation, and scope and resource scarcity? The answer is no. Policies and arrangements that were adequate for the start-up phase would be seriously inadequate for a mature program.

Four implementation issues threaten the future political, legal, and administrative stability of the employer sanctions program:

Inconsistencies in policy and tactics among different areas of the country and between Border Patrol and INS district office investigators could create serious inequities in the treatment of employers, as similarly situated employers in one INS jurisdiction are treated differently from their counterparts in others. In the long run these inconsistencies could also stimulate internal migration of immigrant-dependent businesses and alien workers. Furthermore, the prevalence of paperwork-only violations and the use of fine quotas raise the age-old legitimacy issue: Is program administration following the letter rather than the spirit of the law? Does it engender respect for the law or contempt for its enforcers? Furthermore, extreme levels of variation across regions and districts give rise to abiding questions of consistency and fairness. Inconsistencies are tolerable, perhaps even desirable, in the short run as ways of developing, testing, and refining approaches to enforcement, but they can destroy legitimacy in the long run if they serve no strategic purpose and alienate the regulated community.

A low level of enforcement activity could lead many employers to discount the possibility that violations will be detected and punished, thus weakening the deterrent effect of employer sanctions. At the program's inception, publicity about the new law and business's uncertainty about the INS's strategy provided the Agency's enforcement efforts with great leverage. That leverage could decline sharply if businesses learn to calculate their chances of being inspected or penalized.

Arbitrary use of criminal sanctions under both pattern and practice and harboring and transporting provisions-- e.g., charging first-time violators with pattern and practice violations--could lead to crippling legal challenges.

Failure to develop strong investigative capabilities will limit the INS's effectiveness in dealing with the most heavily immigrant-dependent employers. In many cities, the most immigrant-dependent firms are small and mobile and are in industries with low barriers to entry. Enforcement can reach them only if investigators have good systems for tracking and monitoring the proprietors. In the short run, it has been possible to reach some of these firms through apprehended aliens, but in the long run such an undisciplined and haphazard approach would prove inadequate. Furthermore, fraud and other evasion techniques can be expected to grow more sophisticated as enforcement is stepped up and could require the introduction of comparably sophisticated investigative techniques to defeat them.

RECOMMENDATIONS

These conclusions suggest a number of emphases for future implementation.

Increase Central Oversight of Policy. IRCA establishes the INS as a federal regulatory agency administering a national regime of regulation that applies to all U.S. employers. The penalty structure embedded in IRCA is a cumulative one, with multiple violations over time leading beyond administrative penalties to criminal actions.

Administration of such a scheme will certainly require increased and more systematic reporting of enforcement actions, criteria, and outcomes, and will necessitate greater monitoring of local policy implementation by national administrators. This monitoring is necessary to ensure consistency when appropriate, to promote "best practices" across the country, and to track emerging patterns of compliance.

It also appears that greater clarity should be brought to policies regarding what constitutes an "egregious" violation, the circumstances in which purely paperwork violations should lead to penalties, and criteria for seeking criminal sanctions under the pattern and practice and harboring and transporting provisions. In general, policies regarding the use or threat of criminal sanctions should be clarified and subject to continual monitoring and reexamination to ensure that such sanctions are not invoked unless the employer's intentional violation of the law is unambiguously demonstrated.

Increase Resources Dedicated to Investigative Activity. The shift to regulatory law enforcement should be better reflected in the INS's budget, where interdiction rather than investigation activity continues to consume most Agency resources. This balance should be altered and can be accomplished in one of two ways. Resources dedicated to the Investigations branch can be substantially increased or the Border Patrol could dedicate a larger share of its resources and manpower to investigative activity.

Coordinate Local Enforcement. The Border Patrol's investigative work related to employer sanctions should be rigorously coordinated with INS district offices to ensure that targeting, investigations, and penalty strategies are similar. This coordination should be reinforced by national leadership.

Reinforce the Legitimacy of Targeting Strategies. Despite local INS resistance to the use of neutral targeting strategies, the approach should be sustained to preserve the legitimacy of the enforcement effort, deflect charges of selective enforcement, and detect leakage from industries and labor markets where undocumented labor has historically been dominant. A clear policy on the appropriate treatment of employers who are first-time violators is also needed. Using warnings, not fines, for first-time violators will demonstrate that the INS is interested in deterring illegal immigration rather than inflating enforcement figures by entrapping employers.

Each of these conclusions points to the need to further develop a deliberate national strategy of enforcement that is based on a more complete understanding of the relationship of enforcement to compliance. At minimum, this argues for a systematic follow-up of targets of enforcement actions to determine the longitudinal deterrent effect of varying enforcement strategies. Over time, results from such a monitoring effort could help the Agency make more informed decisions about allocating resources between border and interior enforcement, the emphasis to be placed on citing technical versus substantive violations, and the most productive targets for future enforcement activity.

In the final analysis, however, a strong central office will be required if it appears that resources should be allocated in a manner that disturbs traditional distributional patterns within the Agency.